Radius

Radius

A Story of
Feminist Revolution

Yasmin El-Rifae

VERSO

London • New York

First published by Verso 2022
© Yasmin El-Rifae 2022

1 3 5 7 9 10 8 6 4 2

Verso
UK: 6 Meard Street, London W1F 0EG
US: 388 Atlantic Avenue, Brooklyn, NY 11217
versobooks.com

Verso is the imprint of New Left Books

ISBN-13: 978-1-83976-768-5
ISBN-13: 978-1-83976-770-8 (UK EBK)
ISBN-13: 978-1-83976-771-5 (US EBK)

British Library Cataloguing in Publication Data
A catalogue record for this book is available from the British Library

Library of Congress Cataloging-in-Publication Data

Names: El-Rifae, Yasmin, author.
Title: Radius : a story of feminist revolution / Yasmin El-Rifae.
Description: London ; New York : Verso, 2022.
Identifiers: LCCN 2022020544 (print) | LCCN 2022020545 (ebook) | ISBN
   9781839767685 (hardback) | ISBN 9781839767715 (US ebk) | ISBN
   9781839767708 (UK ebk)
Subjects: LCSH: Operation Anti-Sexual Harassment (Organization) | Sex
   crimes—Egypt—Prevention. | Women—Crimes against—Egypt—Prevention. |
   Feminism—Egypt—History—21st century. | Women political
   activists—Egypt. | Egypt—History—Protests, 2011-2013.
Classification: LCC HV6593.E84 E57 2022 (print) | LCC HV6593.E84 (ebook)
   | DDC 364.15/30962 —dc23/eng/20220617
LC record available at https://lccn.loc.gov/2022020544
LC ebook record available at https://lccn.loc.gov/2022020545

Typeset in Fournier by MJ & N Gavan, Truro, Cornwall
Printed and bound by CPI Group (UK) Ltd, Croydon CR0 4YY

Contents

Introduction

It's summer in New York, and the baby-to-be is growing but does not show in the dark blue dress I'm wearing. A famous writer and his wife, sitting across the table from me at a dinner party, ask me what my book is about.

I say it's the story of a group that fought circles of men that attacked women over and over again while a revolution struggled to survive. The man, the writer, wants to know how this could happen, why. The woman looks at me closely, and says, "It's not the same, not the same at all, but I've felt something like that. At parties and dances, even back at school. Suddenly something would shift, you'd feel a circle forming around you, and I don't know, it's not the same, but there would suddenly be this menace, this threat, grabbing."

I am standing in Adam's apartment in Cairo talking to Leila, whom I haven't seen in two years, and she is telling me that she can no longer dance at weddings or parties, in case a circle forms on the dance floor.

"It's totally irrational, but I just can't."

The space and time between Cairo and New York collapses. Mid-conversation, mid-thought.

Could it happen again? Will it ever not?

The world shows us, over and over again, that we are still being attacked. The story differs depending on who and where you are —rape on campus, domestic abuse, femicide, honor killing. Language changes, new waves of feminism are commodified, battle lines shift, laws improve and regress, but the violence and the threat of it are still there.

At least sometimes when we fight back we don't have to do it alone.

This story is about a feminist intervention group that formed in late 2012, nearly two years into the Egyptian revolution, when mass sexual assaults of female protesters were spreading through Cairo's Tahrir Square.

Reports of mob attacks against female protesters first appeared online. Witnesses and survivors described different levels of violence but it always seemed to start the same way: a group of men would encircle a woman, or multiple women, and from there the crowd would grow to dozens, sometimes hundreds of people. Men groped, stripped, beat, and raped women. Within the chaos of the mob around them, people fought with one another. They pickpocketed. They tried to film what was happening on their phones. Some tried to help the victims, others joined in assault.

The revolution that had erupted so unexpectedly in 2011—a revolution with all of the transcendence and promise of unstoppable, fear-breaking collective action against decades of police brutality, dictatorship, and corruption—was now in a state of political and spiritual crisis. After Hosni Mubarak stepped down in February 2011, the military led a transitional period marked by continued state violence against prodemocracy protesters. In the spring of 2012, the Muslim Brotherhood, the most organized opposition group in the country (despite being legally banned for nearly half a century), won the first open presidential elections. Once in power, the Brotherhood abandoned the revolution's demands, pursuing its own economic and political agenda, seeing little need to make or keep allies. The movement that saw Tahrir Square as its center was now reactive, no longer moving public imagination as much as trying to hold ground, to not let go.

When the attacks against women spread, the dominant feeling among many activists was that they were premeditated. Security forces have a history of paying thugs to harass female protesters, although it had never happened on this scale. Some thought perhaps the Brotherhood was attempting to undermine street-based opposition to their government by paying men to attack women protesters. Or perhaps it was sabotage by formerly powerful members of the security apparatus who were ousted along with Mubarak.

Whatever the cause, women in Tahrir were in increasing danger of being attacked, and no one was doing anything about it until a few groups of people—many of us women who were ourselves attacked or had seen other women attacked—began to organize.

The group at the center of this book was one of the earliest to form and was organized by activists who could broadly be described as leftist, many of whom already knew and had worked with one another. We started out without a name, going to the protests wearing pink ribbons around our arms so that we could spot one another in the crowds. Everything else grew from there.

We spent a long time debating what to name the group. It wasn't clear which Arabic word to use to describe what we were fighting against—*taharrosh*, the most commonly used word for harassment in Egyptian dialect, didn't capture the violence of the attacks. Back then, *taharrosh* could mean catcalling or teasing; it was understood to be potentially harmless. We decided on the long but more accurate Operation Anti–Sexual Harassment and Assault, Opantish for short. With the name came Facebook and Twitter pages, and T-shirts that became our uniform with the motto "A Midan Safe for All" printed in Arabic on the back. (*Midan* means both traffic circle and public square in Arabic. Throughout the revolution it was commonly used to refer to Tahrir, a major traffic circle in downtown Cairo, which was transformed into a public square when it was occupied by protesters. I have chosen to use it in transliterated form throughout this book when referring to Tahrir.)

We created a sophisticated operational structure that, at its peak, deployed hundreds of volunteers working in specialized teams on the ground. Men and women learned how to effectively fight their way into the mobs, packed first aid material and spare clothes to carry on their backs for victims, debated whether to carry weapons. Getaway drivers mapped the best routes for avoiding military barricades when they were driving women away. In the press, we talked about the state's long history of complicity in sexual violence against women, called out leftist activists and political groups for ignoring or even denying the ongoing attacks (*this isn't the time for women's issues*, they said), and organized ourselves around an unapologetic discourse: women had a right to be in the square any time we pleased, we were not to be separated or cordoned off from political action on the street, we had a right to both speak about and fight this violence.

From physically intervening on the ground to overseeing the complicated logistics of the operation, women led. Opantish positioned itself as a necessary part of the revolution even as it struggled against sexism within revolutionary circles.

Everything that follows is based on interviews and conversations with other organizers of the group, email correspondence and news reports from the time, and my own notes and memories. Some names and some details have been changed for privacy. This is just one telling of a very real history; within and around it, there are countless others.

Part I

Whatever it is that you write in this book, I'll always have a problem with it. Because I'll always be looking for the gaps between what you've written and what I remember.

—Farida, 2018

There are certain memories which remain inviolate to the ravages of time. And to those of suffering. It is not true that everything is colored by time and suffering. It is not true that they bring everything to ruin.

—Han Kang, *The White Book*, 2016

1

January 25, 2013

11:00 a.m.

In her living room, T took the newly printed T-shirts out of the plastic bags they'd come in. She held one up and ran her fingers along the curled letters stenciled into red block on the front. "Against Assault" the text said in Arabic.

Farida had designed the logo a couple of weeks ago, in this same room. "It has to be strong and simple," she'd said, her brow scrunched as her fingers moved on the mouse pad.

There were seventy-five T-shirts for T to take to the intervention teams. As she packed them into a black duffel bag, she wondered how many people would actually show up.

She went into her bedroom and opened her closet. A blue Post-it note that had been stuck to the closet door lost the last of its glue and fluttered to the ground. A note from Adam—"Buy lightbulbs!"—in his small, meticulous cursive.

She liked the marks that were left by people and by the work that they did together. Her apartment was on the eleventh floor of a building just a few blocks away from Tahrir Square, and for the past two years the place had been totally open to the world that was changing outside. People worked in her living room, sometimes on her balcony. It had functioned as a meeting space for nascent political initiatives, a hideout, a refuge. On her fridge, on the walls, underneath her bed were sketches that later became posters, maps of protest routes, drawings and doodles made during conversations. There were T-shirts and scarves and hoodies belonging to various friends that were mixed up in her own wardrobe. People slept in her bed and cooked in her kitchen. Nahya kept a pair of pajama pants here.

T took off her jeans and pulled on a pair of long johns, and on top of them a blue one-piece swimsuit. A base layer of protection, hard to remove, impossible to rip. She pulled the straps over her shoulders, feeling the tightness around her chest. The restriction, normally uncomfortable, was now reassuring. She put a black tank top on over it, then her T-shirt.

She pulled her jeans back on over the long johns–swimsuit combination.

She planned to be with the so-called safety teams who take care of survivors once they had been pulled out of a mob. They were supposed to stand near the intervention teams, but to stay on the outside of the crowd, to not get pulled into the fighting. But T had learned to be ready just in case—things changed quickly, and she didn't want to find herself unprepared.

Her worn-out old Nikes would come off too easily. She reached in the back of her closet for a pair of heavy boots she hardly ever wore.

Then she went to the mirror, thinking about her hair. A ponytail would be too easy to pull, an obvious target. She could pin it up and tie a scarf around it, pirate-style. Yes, that will do. At night, she'd pull the hood of her hoodie on too.

"*AL-DAKHLIYYA! BALTAGIYYA!*" (Cops are thugs!) The unmistakable rhythmic sound of chanting voices suddenly filled her bedroom. It was earlier than usual: Friday prayers had not even begun. It sounded like a small group, perhaps too eager to wait for the day's activity to kick off. The sound moved past her, on its way, she assumed, to Tahrir.

It had been two years since mass protests broke out in 2011. Just like that, when they least expected it, when the stasis and corruption and police brutality underneath a veneer of slick neoliberal reforms had all but hollowed out any sense of imagination or political possibility, *it* was here, an actual revolutionary upheaval that threw Hosni Mubarak out of his thirty-year presidency.

In the two years of ongoing, leaderless protest, Tahrir remained the symbolic heart of the revolution. It was here that the first marches headed on January 25, and it was here that they returned three days later, after 100 police stations were burnt to the ground around the country, after the government's attempts to stop what had begun—including shutting down cell phone lines and the internet—did nothing to stop millions more from coming out into the street. Through each victory and each setback since, the feeling was that if Tahrir was lost, the whole dream of change would be lost with it. The way the revolution had become the center of T's life, had become her life, was matter of fact, inevitable.

She looked at her outfit. Good enough.

12:00 p.m.

Marwan's alarm clock, which he had put on a dresser across the room, was getting louder, rising to an unreasonable blare.

He felt like there were weights on his eyelids. How had the night already passed? It was late by the time he'd gotten home from base the night before, but that wasn't why it was so hard to get up. He had been sleeping so deeply recently that it scared him a little. When he woke up in the mornings, he felt like he was dragging his limbs through water.

He was lucky to be able to sleep at home, to have regular weekends in the city. When he was conscripted into the army his parents had used their connections to get him an administrative post where he could use his engineering degree and have soft hours.

He was due to meet Seif at 3:00 p.m.

"We need you to be a team captain," Seif had said on the phone.

"OK," Marwan said. "But I thought you already had two captains."

"Yes, but we need at least four. We're going to try and have four teams on the ground, one at each corner of the square," Seif said. "You can do it, right, it'll be your day off?"

Marwan had no particular skill or advantage in street fighting. Since the revolution began, he'd blustered his way through clashes with the police, throwing rocks, learning to take cover and deal with tear gas just like everyone else. That was the extent of his experience with violence, with fighting, with crowds. Seif had called him only because he knew him well enough to trust him. The intervention group had only been around for a couple of months, since last November, when the attacks against women in the square started becoming a pattern. They were still figuring out who could do what.

He opened the balcony doors and stepped out into the Friday quiet. Cars were parked tight against each other along the curve of the street. In another time, this would have been a day for reading or for working on his screenplay.

He changed out of his boxers and into a tight pair of briefs. He reached for his jeans and then decided to put the boxers on over the briefs first, clenching at the memory of fingers that felt surprisingly pointy as they scratched and pried at his asshole in the crush the last time he went out to volunteer.

He pulled on a black long-sleeved T-shirt, put on his belt in case it would be useful later. He stopped at the mirror.

He knew he could make himself look more frightening, like a combination of a thug and a police officer. He had the shape for it—his face was angular, his complexion slightly dark. His body still carried some of the athleticism of his school years, even though he'd stopped playing sports or working out. He knew he could add to his natural authority on the street by changing his voice, his walk, and the look in his eyes.

He put a black bandana in his pocket, grabbed his keys and cigarettes and was out the door.

Around twenty-five people had gathered at the meeting point for the intervention teams, on the slip road in front of the Arab League building right off Tahrir Square, a road concealed by a metal fence and some trees. Someone had made friends with the guard and he let them use the road, technically off-limits to pedestrians, as a meeting point.

Marwan spotted Seif, wearing his usual black T-shirt and black shorts that reached past his knees, a hoodie slung over one shoulder. He was thin and wore his hair slicked back in a ponytail. He was standing with Leila, whose hands were moving emphatically as she spoke, her shoulders high and stiff. By the time Marwan reached them, they had sorted out whatever it was they were disagreeing about; Seif greeted him with his crooked smile and embraced him.

"So far we've only got enough people for two teams, with twelve people each," Seif said. "You'll take Team 2, you guys will be stationed near Hardee's. I'll take the other team, and we'll stay on the opposite side of the midan."

"OK. And have we got scouts?" Marwan asked.

"We've put some eyes on two balconies, one off of Simón Bolívar Square and the other near KFC. And there's someone in the operations room whose job is to sit on the balcony and monitor."

Leila turned to the ten people who made up Marwan's team. "We should take a minute for everyone on the team to introduce themselves to one another, and then both teams should also meet. We should all know each other's faces."

There were three women on the team, including Leila.

"Let's wait and see if more people turn up," Leila said. "I'll go with whichever team has less women."

They were still introducing themselves when T showed up, carrying a large duffel bag.

"How many T-shirts do you need?" she asked Marwan. "Thirteen," he said.

She counted them out and made a note on a clipboard.

She handed him and Seif a cell phone each. "Here, so your own phones don't get stolen. We've put in the numbers of the other captains and most of the people in the operations room."

She passed Marwan an empty tote bag. "You can use this for the watches and keys and whatever else people don't want to take with them. We'll keep it in the operations room and we can give everything back to people at the end of the night." The men in Team 2 already knew not to wear valuable watches, and the women didn't wear jewelry.

"Keep your IDs in your pockets," Marwan said to his team as he put his keys in the bag. He didn't say *in case we get arrested*, because he believed that was understood.

T picked up the bag full of unused T-shirts, its weight an indication of how few people had shown up. Maybe more would come later in the evening.

4:00 p.m.

The operations room was Pierre's apartment, a sprawling space with a balcony that ran around the entire front side of the building, directly overlooking the midan. Several of the now iconic images of Tahrir full of protesters, tents, and promise in the early days of the uprising had been photographed from there.

By early afternoon, the square had begun to fill with people gathering to commemorate the second anniversary of the January 25 revolution. In the last two years, a new calendar had emerged of anniversaries of street battles and of massacres by the police and the military, and the memory of those who had been killed brought a sharp, hot anger to the protests and marches commemorating each event. January 25 marked the day when this period of possibility and counterrevolutionary violence had begun. It did not matter that the Muslim Brotherhood—long banned but grudgingly tolerated during Mubarak's final decade—had won the presidency in elections a few months earlier. The institutional apparatus responsible for state violence—for the torture and murder of detainees in the years of Mubarak, for the shooting and kidnapping of protesters since 2011—had retreated but was still intact. Despite the Brotherhood's win, there had been no accountability for past violence, no transition to a new police or justice system.

Now protesters in the midan lifted up large white banners bearing the stenciled faces of those who'd fallen: the young Mina Daniel, run over by a tank and killed with twenty-eight other Coptic Christians; Sheikh Emad Effat, shot by police; the forever-sixteen-year-old Jeeka, whose face was captured in mid-chant, his mouth forming an almost perfect O, its stillness strange and graceful on the rippling banners.

On my way up to the operations room I ran into Habiba, her

arms full of shopping bags, bundles of empty backpacks hanging off of each shoulder.

"Give me some of those," I said, and we made our way up in the elevator, plastic crinkling between us.

We walked into the central living room and put everything down on the floor. She pointed her head toward a row of backpacks leaning against the wall and said, "Those ones over there are from last time, from December. We should repack them and see what's missing."

She held up an *abaya* (a floor-length robe, usually black, worn by conservative women). "Man, look at this, these are the plainest ones I could find in that shitty Tawheed wal Nour store." The robe was black with large sequined flowers running down the front. "There were a lot of sequins, and *a lot* of leopard print trims," she said.

On a small whiteboard in the corner of the room, I wrote out the list:

SAFETY KITS:
UNDERWEAR
ABAYAS
FLIP FLOPS
GAUZE + TAPE + BETADINE
PANADOL

We sat on the floor and began sorting the materials by item. Nahya walked in, her face tense and serious, almost angry. She was wearing jeans and an Opantish T-shirt that hung down to her knees.

"I have the hotline phones. And someone gave me these to store up here," she said as she set down a case of Pyrosol bug spray, which people were using to light flares, to clear space in the crowds.

"Do you have the cell phones? Are they charged?" Habiba asked her.

"Yes, and there's one Mobinil, one Etisalat, one Vodafone, so hopefully at least one will work if the networks jam." She put them on the dining table, in a row. Next to them was a stack of flyers.

OPERATION ANTI SEXUAL HARASSMENT & ASSAULT
Mass sexual assaults of women have plagued Tahrir Square.

If you see an assault, call one of these numbers:
01231242471, 0100985432, 0134789321

This is our midan, and we won't leave it.

"I have to go start distributing these, but the rest of the midan team isn't here yet," she said, irritated. "Let me help you first."

We started packing in a sort of assembly line, two types of item in front of each of us. Nahya turned over a pair of blue cotton underwear in her hands, as though it were a strange new object, before she packed it in the backpack and passed it over to me.

"We've run out of Panadol," I said.

"Shit, I thought we had more left over from last time," Habiba said. "We've got to start keeping an inventory. OK, I'll call one of the runners."

"We have runners?" Nahya asked.

It didn't take long for the three of us to pack a dozen safety kits. We put them back against a wall, keeping the ones missing the painkillers separate.

Once we'd finished, Nahya went downstairs to make more photocopies of the flyers. The guy in the shop behind the old

American University campus wanted to charge her an extortionate fifty piasters per page. "No one else will even be open now," he said.

He changed his tone when she showed him the flyers and told him what they were for. "If I could afford it, I swear I'd give them to you for free," he said. "But you know, it's been hard since the American University moved to New Cairo."

Nahya walked to the midan, which was slowly filling up. There was a stage to one side, where politicians, revolutionary groups, and the relatives of martyrs were expected to give speeches later in the day. A few families hung around the central circle, with children sitting at the edge, their legs dangling off the curb. Face painters, their own faces covered in the red, white, and black of the Egyptian flag, roamed about, carrying jars of paint and brushes.

In the first weeks of the uprising, Nahya had slept here every night, both exhausted and exhilarated. Even as she'd gone on television ahead of the first protests and talked about why they needed to happen, why the regime needed to change, she hadn't imagined anything on the scale of a mass uprising—she'd thought they'd have a day of smallish protests, get kettled and beaten up by the cops, maybe there would be a few arrests, and then it would be over, the same kind of confrontation they'd been having for the last few years. But once the January movement started, it kept going, and she had wanted to be in the center of it, here in the square, organizing different tents with different functions, trying to understand the political changes that were happening so quickly, the organized fronts and alliances that were forming, ignoring Western journalists' phone calls, tweeting occasionally. She had never thought, then or even a few months ago, that one day her relationship with the square would become about fighting gang rape.

She stopped at a group of three women and a man, who were all carrying flags. When they saw she had flyers with her, they reached out their hands.

"We're a group that's intervening in the mob harassment that's been happening to women in the square," she said. "Call these numbers if you see anything. There will be women and men wearing T-shirts like this one"—she tugged at the front of her own—"and they'll be here, if you need help or if you see something."

"There's no harassment here!" the man said emphatically, almost shouting. "If anything like that happened, we'd take care of it!" But the two women looked at Nahya and nodded, folded the flyers up, and put them in their pockets.

5:00 p.m.

The intervention teams were scheduled to be in the square at 7:00 p.m., an hour after dark, but the hotlines had already started ringing. Habiba picked up the first call.

"I need some harassment," a guy said, the sound of the street behind him. She could hear the people around him laugh.

The next call was from a woman, and her voice was shaking down the line but she spoke quickly, urgently: "A group surrounded me and my friends and they started grabbing us, but then a guy drove a motorbike into the crowd, I think he was trying to help us by breaking things up. We were able to get away," she said.

"Are you safe? Do you need anything?" Habiba asked.

"We're in a café and we're fine, we just wanted to let you know that this happened."

On the paper in front of her, Habiba logged the call under "no intervention."

She put the phones in her pockets and went out to look at

the square. Arwa was standing on the other end of the balcony, looking down through her binoculars. "Come look at this," she said.

Right beneath them at the beginning of Talaat Harb Street, a thick crowd was moving into the square. It was mostly men but toward the front of it, near the iron rail on the pavement, they could see a woman. The crowd around her looked tighter, and there was a lot of movement, but it was impossible to see what was actually happening.

"Shit, the intervention teams aren't even here yet," Habiba said.

The light was starting to fade, and from the far end of the square they could hear chants. "Justice for the martyrs!" protesters cried from below the banners.

5:30 p.m.

T and Arwa stood on the balcony, watching the square below. The crowd they'd spotted half an hour earlier had dispersed and now a new one was moving—with surprising speed—toward the old Nile Hilton, on the opposite side of Tahrir. Then it changed direction and came down the square toward them.

Arwa picked up her video camera and followed it. It stopped at the juice shop a block away from them, swarmed in place for a few minutes. "I can't see any woman," she said. "Maybe she's inside the shop?"

"I'll go down in case someone's in there," T said.

"I don't think it's a good idea," Arwa said, looking up from her camera.

But the crowd was breaking up. The people in it—there must have been about sixty of them—were no longer one mass. "Look, they've gone," T said. "I'll get someone to go with me."

She grabbed a safety kit and rushed down to the lobby. There were half a dozen volunteers standing around, and one of them offered go with her.

In the shop, a man was sitting on a plastic chair, watching a television. He looked up at them and then back at the screen.

"Was a woman brought in here just now from outside?" T asked him.

"She's not here anymore, they took her," he said, looking at T now.

"Took her where?"

(The smell of overripe oranges, of the sawdust on the floor.)

"I don't know," the man said, shrugging his shoulders.

"Who took her? Anyone wearing a T-shirt like these?" T asked.

"There's no one here, lady," he said and turned back to the television.

They went back outside and saw that a mass of people was moving toward Bab al-Louk Street.

"Come on," T said, and she started running toward it.

As T and the volunteer pushed their way in, she used her elbows to make space around her. When the crowd moved in any direction it was a struggle to stay upright. She couldn't see past the back of the person in front of her, and if she stood on her tiptoes her balance gave way in the heaving crush. No one was really looking at her, and she didn't want to draw attention to herself yet by using her voice, so she just pressed on, elbowing her way through bit by bit.

When she reached the woman in the middle, she was not making a sound. Her face was frozen still, her mouth was closed. But her eyes would not stop moving in circles, darting fast around their sockets.

A man standing behind her had his arm around her shoulders, and he, like everyone around them, was shouting, "Get away from her!"

T tried to convince him to let her be the one to hold onto the woman, but he was adamant that he would not let her go. He had one arm around the woman's shoulders and was using his free arm to push the crowd away.

"OK, OK, let me hold on to her, and you hold on to me. Let the women stick together, it's better."

He agreed to this. T put her hands on the woman's shoulders, facing her, and told her, "I'm with you, I'm with you." After the fourth or fifth time she said it, the woman finally looked at her.

The shouting around them continued.

"We'll wait for an ambulance here!"

"No, we'll take them to Shabrawy!"

T had no idea where the other volunteer had gone. But so far, these men were helping them, and this woman's eyes had locked on to hers and stopped their panicked whirl.

6:30 p.m.

The hotlines rang relentlessly.

"They tried to pull me into a microbus on Tahrir street."

"I see a woman being attacked near KFC. She's naked ... completely naked."

Habiba relayed information to the captains, to whomever she could get through to, and tried to keep a record of the calls coming in. Her hands stayed wrapped around the cell phone after each call, unable to let go.

"I have a group of guys here with me, we can help you, tell us what to do."

"There's a mob in front of Hardee's, I think there's a woman inside, she's crushed against the iron rail, you need to send someone quick!"

7:00 p.m.

There was no time between attacks. Marwan's team had just put a woman in a car at the museum corner of Tahrir, when they heard there was something else happening across the square. He ran, pushing his way past people, shouting at them to get out of the way. His Opantish T-shirt had been ripped in a neat diagonal from his shoulder down the front and hung in an open flap down his chest. He hadn't seen the knife.

He could see the mob in front of Hardee's and the bright red of Peter's bandana, a head taller than everyone around him. The streetlight at the corner had gone dark. He couldn't see into the crowd but he pushed his way toward Peter.

Peter didn't hear him when he called his name. Everyone was shouting and Marwan was stopped for a moment by a man waving a stick around and cursing, "You motherfuckers!" at everybody. Someone punched him in the shoulder from behind and he stumbled forward. When he stood up straight again, Peter punched him in the side of his head. He understood immediately that Peter hadn't recognized him—he wasn't even looking at him. All Peter knew was that those wearing his uniform were on his side, and everyone else was probably not. Marwan, in his black T-shirt, was one of the crowd, a threat to be neutralized and kept away. He was no use like this; he needed an Opantish T-shirt.

He started running toward the operations room but then he spotted a slight guy in the white and bright red of the new uniform T-shirts, a new young volunteer whose name he didn't know. He was facing away from the mob, perhaps pretending not to see what was going on just a few feet away.

Marwan ran up behind him, grabbed the guy by the shoulder and said, "Give me your T-shirt, now, right now."

The kid had fear in his eyes. He didn't say anything but he didn't move.

"Didn't you hear me?" Marwan shouted.

The guy took the T-shirt off and gave it to Marwan without looking him in the eye. Marwan felt relief and tried not to show it when he saw that the boy was wearing another shirt underneath. He pulled the T-shirt on and ran back to Peter and the mob.

Less than a block away, inside Shabrawy, T was still holding on to the woman she'd found in the mob, whose name she still didn't know because she still wasn't speaking.

There were about fifty men crammed into the shop, and they were all shouting.

"Sit over here!"

"No, don't let her sit near the window, move her back here!"

There were two other women on the other side of the shop, and they seemed to be the sister and mother of the silent woman. They were each having completely different reactions to what was happening. The sister let out long, wordless screams, while the mother cried.

T and the other women were being manhandled and pushed and pulled as the men argued. No one was speaking to any of them except to order them where to go.

All T wanted was to gather the women in one spot, check them for injuries, and then to keep them all together, but the men wouldn't let her move. She wasn't able to think because it was so loud with shouting, and each suggestion or plan made by the men around her triggered a new set of possible disasters to worry about.

"WE'LL PUT THEM IN A MICROBUS!"

"WE'LL GO TO THE METRO!"

She still had no idea if any of her teammates knew where she was. Her cell phone, still with her, had no reception. If she could just gather them together and think for a minute, she could come up with something. She began shouting too: "I don't want anyone to lay a finger on any woman here! Bring them here, they're a family, let them stick together!"

To her surprise, her voice, the difference of it, made the men all stop and turn to her. They were silent for a long moment, but the way they looked at her made her think, *What have I done?*

T backtracked. "Look, we're all women, let us be together, and let me just see if they need anything," she said.

"SHE'S HERE TO HELP THEM, MAN, JUST PUT THE WOMEN TOGETHER AND WE'LL SEE WHAT WE'LL DO."

They brought the other two women over and they all sat at a table. (On it, a half-eaten sandwich and a plate of pickles.) They weren't injured but the mother was crying. She learned that the first woman she'd found was named Mona, and her sister was Mai. Mai had stopped screaming but was in a verbalized panic. "How are we going to get out of here?" she asked over and over again.

The owner of the shop had had enough. "Get this crazy shit out of here! That's it, all of you, all of you, out, now!"

The shouting started again.

"WE'VE CALLED A MICROBUS TO COME AND GET THEM!"

Mai cried out, "I'm not getting into a microbus! Who knows where they'll take us or what they'll do! I'll only get in an ambulance!"

"You're right, you're right," T said. "We won't do anything you don't want to do."

She tried to call Seif but she couldn't get a connection.

She had to do *something*.

She raised her voice above the men again. "I've spoken to my group," she shouted. "They've called an ambulance and it will be here in ten minutes. If it's not, then we'll get in the microbus. Ten minutes, just give us ten minutes."

All she could do was buy time.

8:00 p.m.

I was running toward the corner of Hardee's where Peter and his team were meant to be, a safety kit on my back, when I saw them walking quickly down the pavement toward the operations room. His T-shirt was covered in dirt. Next to him was someone whose face was so contorted by anguish that I did not recognize it at first. The person was a woman with dark hair, she was wearing a man's blue sweater, she was holding the waist of her jeans, and she was walking quickly next to Peter but there was a distance between them. It was Farida, and a few steps behind her was Sherine, both new friends to me.

We went into the building, and Farida sat on the stairs, curled over her knees and cried. Sherine was pressing the elevator button over and over again, but her face was stoic, as though carved out of stone. Peter stood to the side and, gesturing toward Farida, said, "Do something, do something for her."

I sat down next to her and she slid down the step, away from me, and said, "No, no touching, please, no touching." She was crying hard.

"Do something," Peter said again.

When the elevator finally arrived, Farida, Sherine, and I got in, and Peter went back out into the square. On our way up, Sherine was staring straight ahead out of the glass doors.

When we went inside a few people came toward us, uncertain

of what had happened, what to do. Farida, still shaking her head, crying, went to Nahya on the balcony.

Something in Sherine's brow had changed. She said, "I need to go check myself," and headed toward the bathroom in the hallway.

She drew the bathroom door behind her, left it open a crack. I could hear her crying now that she was finally alone. I sat down outside the bathroom door, unsure whether going inside would be an intrusion. "I'm here," I said. "I won't come inside unless you ask me to. I'm here."

This was no longer the same space where people had assembled safety kits a few hours before. More and more women were coming up, in injury and shock and loss. There was blood and tears and *Where is my sister, she was standing beside me, where is she, I held on to her for as long as I could.*

The people who brought them upstairs—the people wearing Opantish T-shirts—were hurt too. They talked about blades and guns and how no one was prepared and it had never been like this, no one ever thought it could be.

The plan had collapsed. There were not enough people on the ground, and the attacks were relentless. The crowds—the mobs—were too big. The team captains' phones didn't work or they'd been stolen. People were constantly getting separated from one another.

A woman came into the apartment. Her trousers were gone. Tied around her waist were two sweatshirts that people must have given her, one in the front and one in the back. She was barefoot and there was dirt on her arms and her legs, her feet covered in black. Her hair was a mess. But she moved calmly through the apartment next to a volunteer who brought her to me with a panicked look on his face. "I don't know what to do for her," he said.

I took her into a room where there were extra supplies.

"How about these?" I said, holding up a pair of loose black cotton trousers.

"Those will fit," she said, pulling them on.

I handed her a pair of flip-flops, and realized that was the last of what I had to offer her. As we went back outside, she looked at me and said, "My name is Amy. This is amazing, that this exists."

I started to say, "It's nice to mee—" and my words stopped themselves halfway.

Another organizer walked past us, looking with disbelief at a wad of blood-soaked paper towels that she was carrying. "Where did all this blood come from?" she said to herself out loud.

About ten volunteers sat on the floor, recovering, bandaging wounds. Leila sat alone in a corner of the room, facing the wall, her hands grasping the sides of the chair.

The apartment had turned into some kind of triage unit.

On the balcony a woman, one of the runners, cried because of what had happened to her friend. "It's just, it's *her*, you know?" she said. I put a hand on her shoulder.

There were fireworks in the sky. But below the protesters were gone. The banners of the martyrs were gone. There were no chants. The square was empty of everything except the circles of attack. There were three of them happening at the same time: the circles moving, the arms raised, the screams audible. Arwa pointed her small camera down at hell.

9:00 p.m.

Leila tried to go back outside to rejoin what was left of the intervention teams.

The elevator wasn't working so she ran down the stairs, which wrapped around the open elevator shaft. As she got closer to the ground floor, she heard a clamoring noise rising up, getting louder and louder. The lights on the landing switched off automatically and she hit the switch on the next floor, and then she started to hear the banging, men's shouting voices. She paused when the lobby came into her view.

Volunteers were pushing against the building door from the inside, some of them holding onto a metal bar laced through its handles, pushing against it as if to reinforce its lock. The doorman was standing and pushing with them.

On the other side of the heavy glass doors was a crowd trying to break in.

She texted Habiba: "mob breaking into the building."

She stood next to the doorman and planted her feet on the ground, put her hands on the bar, and pushed with all the weight she could summon.

"They saw women coming up," the doorman said, shouting so she could hear him. "We had to fight them with sticks, but more and more kept coming. I cut the power from the elevator in case they break in. Who are we supposed to call? There's no police, no one to come and help ... we're on our own."

9:15 p.m.

Time had run out for T and the three other women who were stuck in Shabrawy—the owner wanted them out. When the doors opened, T could see Marwan and Seif and more people in white T-shirts. Relief rushed through her.

They were being pushed out of the shop but the movement was slow, there were so many people around them. They had to walk out and around the corner to the ambulance. It was only twenty feet, but the minutes were taking hours. T was behind Mona and her mother, pushing them forward. There were hands everywhere. On T's sides, on her neck, on her thighs, in the waist of her pants, in her underwear, in parts that we call private. There was a finger up her asshole. They—these men who were making such a performance out of helping them—were trying to separate her and the other women. Someone was trying to work the shoulder straps of her backpack off her shoulders, which would mean her hands would have to let go of the woman in front of her. So she turned to the other man behind her, whose finger was in her ass, and shouted, "He's trying to steal my backpack! He's stealing it!"

This man who was assaulting her suddenly turned hero, started yelling, "You motherfucking thief!" at whoever the perpetrator was, fighting him off with one arm while keeping the other in her jeans.

When they reached the ambulance, she couldn't see Marwan or Seif or any of the volunteers. She and the other women half-climbed, were half-pushed by the crowd into the ambulance. Five men she didn't know climbed in with them and then they were driving through the crowds in Tahrir, braking to a halt every few seconds. Each time the car braked, T and the other people in the back flew in different directions, hitting the sides of the ambulance like popping corn. She landed on top of Mona once, she landed on her back another time, and one of the men fell on top of her and kneaded her breasts.

"Stop this screaming!" the ambulance driver yelled back at them.

One of the women's shirts rode up and the driver yelled, "Cover your sister up! Stop this now, otherwise I'll let you all out right here."

The ambulance took them to Qasr al-Ainy Hospital. A pair of doctors at admissions asked the four women,

"Who were the men you're saying attacked you?"

"You mean you didn't know them?"

"Why did you go to the square?"

The family of women decided they didn't want to check in or be examined, so they all walked back outside and T stopped a taxi to take them home. Mona, Mai and their mother had all been robbed of their money, so T gave the driver the cash in her pocket. They drove off, and she stood in front of the hospital facing the Nile, about a mile south of Tahrir. She had to get back to the operations room.

9:30 p.m.

Suddenly, Leila felt the tension on the other side of the building door go slack. She saw people on the other side of the door pulling away, and then they were running down the street.

She heard the pop pop pop pop of the police's tear gas canisters.

Thank god, she (an anarchist atheist) thought.

11:30 p.m.

When T finally got back to the operations room, her relief was so great she felt elated. Triumphant.

Nahya's face was frozen still. "Are you alright?"

"Yeah, it was shit, but I'm fine, I'm OK," T said.

A pause.

"Are you sure?" Nahya asked again.

"What's wrong, why are you looking at me like that?" T asked.

She went to the bathroom and turned on the tap to wash her hands and face. When she looked in the mirror, she saw that her neck, her arms, and the right side of her forehead were covered in bruises that were starting to darken.

Oh, she thought. *Oh.*

Three years later, T said to me in an interview: "It was only then that I realized: it was *me* that was assaulted. That whole time,

I'd thought I was superman. I thought *they* were the victims. What did I have to worry about? I was there to save *them.*"

12:00 a.m.

There weren't many people left in the operations room. I felt like I should stay until everyone else went home, but something inside of me had begun to fray.

Nahya was leaning against a wall, her arms crossed against her chest, looking out at the balcony where Farida was lying down next to a friend, quiet.

"It feels shit being up here," she said. "I know I can't go down, I know I can't actually fight, I'm not ready. But it feels shit being up here."

The square was empty and dark. The police had flooded it with tear gas, and there were young men fighting them with rocks and the occasional Molotov cocktail.

Down in the lobby of the building, people were sitting on the stairs, recovering, breathing through cloth soaked in vinegar. A few young men stood by the door, opening and closing it to people coming in and out.

"Don't go outside now," one of them said to me. I thanked him and then ignored his advice.

As soon as I took a few steps outside, the sting of tear gas made my throat close and I bent over coughing. I ran back to the building. The same young man who had warned me not to leave gave me a piece of cloth soaked in vinegar to breathe through.

Right behind me there was urgent banging on the door of the building, and I could see a red-and-white T-shirt through the thick glass.

It was Marwan and another volunteer I didn't know, whose leg was bleeding. Marwan had his arm around him, half-carried him to the stairs. The man fainted as soon as he sat down. His head rolled back, a sliver of white still visible between his eyelids.

"Vinegar and water, please," Marwan said and I held the soaked cloth up to the man's nose. His jeans were slashed open below the knees, soaked with blood.

"I think he's been hit on the head," Marwan said.

There were ambulances stationed a few blocks away. The medics brought the stretcher into the lobby, and the young man still wasn't awake when they laid him down on it. "His name is Tamer," Marwan said to the medics.

When I went back outside again, guys with scarves wrapped around their faces were walking down the street on jumpy legs, holding rocks, ready to continue their battle with the police. A man yelled to me, "Where are you going?! It's dangerous! You'll get hurt!"

I ignored him and kept walking toward my house. I didn't feel danger here. This was familiar, this adrenaline, this sharpness in the air. I thought could navigate this.

A year earlier, I would have known without question that I was on the side of these people fighting the police. Now I was no long sure how many sides there were, who was on which side, if any of them were on ours. My house was just a few blocks away now, but when I saw a cab, I stopped it.

In the backseat, I saw I'd missed a call from Habiba and dialed back.

"Where are you?" she asked. Her voice was tight.

"In a cab going home, I thought it was better than walking right now."

"Good, yeah, that makes sense," she said.

"Should I come back? What's going on?"

A pause.

"No, no. It's quieted down, people are leaving. The square's still empty. You go to sleep."

"Are you OK? Your voice—"

Her breath caught. When she spoke again her voice was quieter but higher in pitch. She was crying.

"A woman was raped with a knife in the square. Just now."

I can't remember what I felt as I heard this, whether the feeling was hot or cold. I only remember the yellow streetlamps out the window as we drove.

"I'll come back."

"No, no, it's OK," Habiba said. "Nahya's going to the hospital with her. There's nothing else to do right now."

Two days later, we published this press release.

Opantish Press Release, January 27, 2013

On Friday the 25th of January 2013, in the midst of large demonstrations marking the second anniversary of the beginning of the Egyptian revolution, horrific sexual crimes were committed against women in and around Tahrir Square. Operation Anti-Sexual Harassment/Assault (OpAntiSH) received 19 reports of group sexual assaults against women in the area, which included the use of life-threatening violence in some cases. The group was able to intervene in 15 cases, managing to rescue women from the attackers and escort them to safe houses or hospitals to receive the necessary medical attention.

These attacks represent a startling escalation of violence against women in Tahrir Square in terms of the number of incidents and the extremity of the violence which took place. In some cases blades and other weapons were used against women, OpAntiSH volunteers, and other people who tried to intervene. This phenomenon requires urgent attention and treatment, and is linked to the broader social problem of endemic and daily sexual harassment and assault of women.

OpAntiSH expresses extreme disappointment with revolutionary groups and political parties which call for demonstrations in Tahrir square and use the large turnouts for their political bargaining, but neglect their responsibility in securing the square and addressing these repeated sexual assaults against female participants. This reflects a reprehensible attitude of indifference towards violent sexual crimes which aim to terrorize women and prevent them from participating in demonstrations.

Despite the participation of some passersby, OpAntiSH views these assaults as inseparable from the long list of repressive tactics which have targeted Egyptian activists. OpAntiSH stresses that continuing to ignore the dangers women face in the ongoing struggle for justice in this country jeopardizes not only women's participation but the very success of the revolution. At a time when the very presence of women in Tahrir Square carries the same level of risk and danger as approaching the front lines of battle, the women who insist on exercising their rights to participate in demonstrations should be respectfully viewed as a source of courage and inspiration. We are dismayed by the dismissive attitude taken by most political movements to their injuries.

2

Nahya stayed in the hospital for three days with the young woman, whom we'll call Nora. The knife ripped Nora's perineum, cutting her between her vagina and her anus. They didn't know if she would live.

Nora was nineteen years old.

There were other cuts on her body.

Nahya watched silently as the men in Nora's family threw themselves on the hospital floor and wailed in their shame.

"I can make her a girl again," the doctor said. The women in Nora's family asked Nahya if she thought a hymen replacement should be done, as part of the surgery to save her life.

"I think that's Nora's decision," Nahya said.

She tried to stay out of the family's way, never to behave as though her voice was equal to theirs in anything that happened to Nora, in any decisions that needed to be made.

She stayed in Nora's room and talked to her and held her hand when no one else was there. She told her that she was brave.

While they waited for the surgery, Nahya thought about her own hospital stay, after she'd been shot a year earlier. It was a memory of love. Her room had been full all the time, annoying the hospital staff.

"Patients are only allowed four visitors at a time! You all are blocking the hallways! We can't work!"

There was all of her family, from everywhere, and friends close and distant and people she'd met in the midan whose last names she would never know. Soon there were journalists, too, and she had agreed to see a few of them, because what had happened to her then wasn't her story alone, the shotgun pellets that still sat just under her skin could have been for anyone. She could still feel the pellets if she ran her finger over certain parts of her body, she could look at them if she wanted. When they burst into her body, two full rounds, she had fallen in the street but she had felt people carry her, lifting her up and telling her they wouldn't leave her. When she woke up again, really woke up and was past that white place of shock and its dreamlike uncertainty about what was real, she realized she had joined the long list of the revolution's injured protesters. Hers was the apex of righteous bodily injury: bullets from a gun, carried by a cop, shot at her in the night while she filmed a protest.

No one brought Nora flowers. Everyone was focused on hiding the truth of what had happened to her, on hiding the wound, on burying it.

"The neighbors are wondering where she is," Nora's sister said. "They think they smell dishonor."

In the end, the surgeon replaced Nora's hymen without asking her.

"I have made you like you were before," he told her proudly after the operation. Nahya thought his words were cruel—Nora would never be the same, nor should she have to be. But it was the relief on Nora's face at hearing them that made Nahya cry.

Nahya had lived to be a hero. Nora could only live to be a girl.

3

How did this happen? How did people—women and men, but especially women—find it in themselves to use their bodies, to risk their minds, to save strangers? What did they do with their fear?

I took these questions with me when I left Cairo about a year after the revolution ended, after a popular military coup displaced the Muslim Brotherhood government in 2013. The state's massacre of Islamist supporters—killing nearly a thousand people in one day—ensured that those social and political divisions would become an ongoing wound, one that kneecapped any potential for effective opposition to the repression that would define the following years.

I left for the freedom of being somewhere totally new, unbound by anything or anyone, in a place whose limitations and cruelties I did not yet know so well. I wanted to write, but the physical distance did not help with my questions. What had taken place so recently already seemed bizarre, unbelievable. I tried to write the parts that I knew—what the square had felt like, what it smelled like, the way that the urgency of what we were doing took over our lives—but the language was all wrong and my stomach would tie itself in knots, my heart would start racing when I sat at my laptop. I would lie down on the floor of whichever subletted room I was in and wait for my body to calm down.

I had only one answer for our boldness: that it was a time of revolution and rebellion and that this kind of collective action was in the atmosphere. And that was true, of course. The people in the core team who led Opantish were organizers with experience in collective work; they were radical and they saw the work they were doing as the heart of the revolution. But how did this play out for us as individuals moving our bodies and our psyches through such danger?

I started writing to other Opantish organizers to see if they would talk to me on visits back to Cairo. I was shy in the emails, afraid of knocking on doors that people needed to keep closed.

~~I'm working on a book~~

~~I think it's important to document~~

~~I understand if you'd rather not, for any reason.~~

But every person I wrote to wanted to talk, and I would record those interviews over the next four years. I asked everyone I spoke with, especially in the earlier sessions, about fear and how they dealt with it.

Interviews

Lina, 2015: "The first time, I was terrified … I didn't know what was waiting for me. But it wasn't the kind of terror of shaking legs … my legs kept walking forward, I couldn't go back. Once I was inside the circle, once I saw the two women in there, I forgot everything else. And you are so consumed by what you are doing, the need to make spontaneous decisions, one after the other …

afterwards you have no idea how you made them, what you were thinking …"

For many of the people I spoke with, once they'd started and once they'd seen what was happening in those mobs, it was almost impossible to stop so long as they were still physically able to go.

Ahmed was a volunteer who came to play a leading role in the intervention teams. He has a solid physical presence—broad-shouldered and slightly stocky, as though he might be a wrestler or a weight lifter. He tells me that before Opantish he'd had what he describes as a regular kind of knowledge about harassment, as in he knew that it happened, that women had a hard time on the streets. He volunteered for Opantish for the first time on January 25, when he joined one of the safety teams.

During the chaos of that night, Nahya spotted him and said, "What are you doing with the safety teams? Go to intervention right now, they need you!"

Ahmed, 2015: "I followed her orders. And that's how it happened for me. Of course, seeing the attacks is different than hearing about them. The very first case I was involved in, we managed to get the girl out, but then one of the members of the safety team was pulled in. I could see her sitting on the ground, and she was OK, wearing tons of layers, but she didn't want to get up, I think she thought she was safer on the ground. I kept trying to go back in to reach her, but the crowd was so intense I couldn't make it, I would try to move forward but I'd keep getting pushed out. After my fourth try, I saw Peter move in with some of the others and they managed to reach her and pull her out, and the fighting continued around them, knives and … in that moment, inside, I decided that I couldn't continue with this, it was too much for me.

"I stuck around until it was over and they had taken her somewhere else, and I went to just check they were all OK. I had decided to leave after that. As I got closer I could see that she was smiling and talking to people, and this is what changed my mind and made me decide to stay. I thought that if she, the one who had been in the middle of this thing, was able to deal with it, then I'd better stay too."

4

January 26, 2013

Arwa sat in front of one of the desktops in the Mosireen office, about a ten-minute walk through downtown from T's apartment and Tahrir. She put her cigarette out in the empty coffee cup next to the keyboard and reached into her pack of blue L&Ms for another.

"How many views?" Habiba asked.

"105,129," she said. "And MBC, CBC, and Nilesat all want to air it."

The video starts from above the crowd. It zooms in closer and we see the movement there in the middle. A cluster of men are hunched over, huddled around something, moving through the crowd with a speed that seems unlikely. They are trying to get out, to get whatever is between them out.

The camera follows the crowd as it moves to the iron rail on the pavement. It is dark except for some light from the shops, and then—for a flash of a second—the figure of a woman appears. Arwa paused the video, selected a draw tool in Final Cut, and pulled a red circle around this momentary female figure. She lined up the voice-over—her own voice—which tells viewers that there is a woman in this circle.

The crowd's movement over the next few seconds is frantic, constant. Arwa made sure the circle moved with the woman, frame by frame. In some moments she is barely visible, and Arwa has to zoom in and increase the screen's brightness and contrast to find her outline.

A flame moves into the crowd. A man is driving it, holding a propane tank, waving it through to make space around the red circle. A man in a gray hooded sweatshirt waves something in the air, something that catches the light and flicks it back. The space around him empties. Is it a knife? Is he trying to help her?

The red circle has moved under the awning of a shop. A man in a white T-shirt moves into the frame, toward the crowd that has followed the red circle. Then two more men in white, then there is a stream of them, white T-shirts with red letters on the back. They push their way into the crowd, into the shop.

Arwa's camera can't follow them inside. It stays on the chaos on the pavement, the crowd that keeps fighting, keeps moving.

Out of cigarettes, alone now in the office, Arwa typed the Arabic words that appear in white font over the darkness of the video's last frames. "There are many ways you can help us," it reads, followed by the URL for Opantish's Facebook page and email address.

January 27, 2013

A bath. How quaint, Leila thinks. Adam had insisted on it in his gentle, knowing way. So you can keep going." He'd run it for her the way she'd asked him to, a bit hotter than comfortable.

"Do you want me to stay or would you rather be alone?"

She squeezed his hand. "I think I need some time by myself."

So she took off her clothes and felt for the bandage on her backside, on the right. She twisted around to look but she could only see the top of the gash. She walked toward the mirror and then thought better of it. Screw it, what's the point. It had happened, she'd keep it clean and covered with Adam's help. No need to make a thing of it.

She sat down into the hot water.

Her back felt heavy against the end of the tub. She'd slept in fits, stiff in the bed, holding Adam's hand across the space between them, unable to imagine wanting to be touched ever again.

She leaned forward for the soap at the other end of the bathtub, and when she looked down she saw the streaks of pink in the water.

"You're not a victim if you're there by choice. You're not a victim if you're there by choice."

She spoke to herself out loud, her voice low and thick as it bounced off the water, the walls, and the tiled floor.

January 28, 2013

Control Room

- Do we need to move?
- Can we separate hotlines/control desk from survivors? From the volunteers? From other people at the flat? Who should be allowed in and out?
- Shifts for control desk. Too many hours of emotional stress. Need to define clear roles
- Ability to add on new volunteers
- Improve communication with intervention teams

Post-care

- Establishing ongoing psychological counseling for ppl who get harassed

- How to deal with concerns about virginity
- Establishing agreements with drs/clinics/hospitals for medical care
- Establishing possible partnerships to cover medical costs

Internal training/strategies

- Training for us on dealing with victims of sexual assault etc.
- Intervention tools
- Getting more volunteers, talking to political parties, sustainability of volunteers

These were the points we gathered over email in the days after January 25, our agenda for an immediate meeting. Suzy offered to host at her apartment in Garden City, and we sent each other emails and messages about which routes to take and which to avoid in order to get there. Police were camped out behind the mosque off Simón Bolívar Square, between Tahrir and Garden City. They'd been there for weeks. Clashes tended to break out toward midday. Kids, some of them not yet teenagers, some of them barefoot, fought the cops with pieces of broken pavement and Molotov cocktails. In response, the police inevitably used tear gas, sending children running out onto the corniche and the main road with scarves wrapped around their faces.

Garden City is saturated with banks, schools, and embassies. The area was planned in the early twentieth century, with small, meandering streets that often lead pedestrians back the way they came. Popular knowledge says that this was done intentionally, according to the elite, colonial sensibilities of the time—the area is built in concentric circles to keep outsiders from using it as a throughway. The layout is even more confounded by the road blockages and diversions of the US and British embassies, surrounded by security and high concrete barriers that seem to thicken and multiply every year. In the daytime, the neighborhood bustles with the consistent, manic din of city life packed into small streets, and then falls into an eerie silence at night.

As we gathered inside Suzy's apartment, the atmosphere was cluttered and warm. We sat in a circle, some of us on sofas and chairs, others on the floor. A small dining table nearby was loaded with food—cupcakes and quiches and other baked goods. Comfort food.

There was an unspoken agreement not to eat or drink until the talking was over. Someone asked for the points that had been collated over email to guide the meeting. Leila raised her hand in front of her and asked, "But wait, sorry, before we go into the agenda, can we debrief first? Can we go around the room and talk about our experiences, about what happened?"

We spoke in turns.

"I never thought it could be this bad."

"I felt like we were being attacked by everyone, really by everyone."

"What is this hatred? What is this? I don't understand, I don't understand."

Some of us cried as we spoke or listened.

"I tried so hard not to let go of her."

Rana, one of the very early organizers of Opantish, said, "I feel responsible for all the women who went out to volunteer and were then attacked. Is this wrong of us to do? Should women really be on the ground, in this?"

Another woman agreed with her, and the question was put to a vote. Should women be on the ground in intervention teams? Should women fight? We started going around the circle of about twenty people. Four people said no, and then it was Leila's turn.

Leila had a reputation for being militant, well-read, and extremely poised. She was one of the most committed members and organizers of the intervention teams. In a room that was heavy with feeling, she sat up straight, her shoulders back.

But when it was her turn to speak, she started to cry, not tears rolling down her face but a pain that was fighting its way out of her body. Her shoulders shook back and forth, and she covered her face with her hands. The rest of the group was silent.

"Excuse me," she said and stood up and walked to the bathroom.

When she came back and sat down again, she was still crying, but she was in control.

"For me, when we started this it was about women fighting for other women, for ourselves," she said, looking at the floor. "I was willing to accept what happened two nights ago, to face it again, as long as I knew that it was for something bigger, that we would keep going. That it wouldn't be wiped away, dismissed just like that."

She looked up. "Who are we to decide what women should or shouldn't do? Let women decide for themselves."

With a gentle voice, Rana said, "But it's not working. Women are being assaulted over and over again. Volunteers are carrying weapons that they don't know how to use. Maybe we should try a different way … maybe we can continue the work on the ground but also take a case to court, with multiple plaintiffs …"

"I'm sorry but I totally, totally disagree," T said. "What justice system are we going to talk about when women are being raped in the streets? I have barely, barely been able to make it here tonight and I can't believe that we're questioning women's roles in this group."

A chorus broke out against Rana.

"We don't believe in this justice system to begin with."

"This is a feminist group, we can't tell women what to do."

Rana and the three others who had voted no went silent.

The day of that meeting, I edited the English translation of

Farida's testimony, which she had written and posted in Arabic to her Facebook account.

January 2013

My testimony of the group sexual assault that happened to me and has happened to many girls in Tahrir

I am a volunteer in Operation Anti-Sexual Harassment. I joined during the days of the collective rapes that happened in November 2012 during the Mohamed Mahmoud memorial. I thought of myself as someone who was very aware and understood the details of organized group rape that happens in Tahrir and that I was at least mentally prepared—that I needed to act calmly and wisely—but the truth was that the situation was completely beyond my abilities.

On January 25th 2013, I arrived at the "Operations Room" where we prepare first aid bags and take calls. We are divided into different groups, each group responsible for something specific, from the "Midan" group that distributes fliers and asks people if they see any cases of group harassment to call these numbers, to the "Rescue" group that enters the crowd and tries to rescue the girl, to the "Safety" group that tries to provide security and first aid for the girl. But these details aren't important.

The rescue group was supposed to begin working at 7 p.m., but while preparing the rescue bags we received calls asking for us to intervene quickly in a case at the Mogamma in Tahrir. Two other volunteers (a guy and a girl) and I left, running with the rescue bags, which contain clothes (because the first thing these scum do is to cut the girl's clothes) and first aid. We arrived at the Mogamma in Tahrir and didn't see anything. We got news again that we should go to Hardee's because there was a case of harassment happening right then. We ran and arrived at a large group, and screaming at the street corner, and alarming numbers squeezed onto the sidewalk. I was sure the girl was in between these crowds but I didn't see her. The girl I was with and I tried to reach her, but I was surprised when men started yelling and telling us, "You'll get beaten up, you won't get out of here, get out!" Before I could understand their warnings a group of men cornered us. To our backs was a *foul* cart, and I didn't understand how suddenly there were not less than five pairs of hands grabbing my chest and cramming their hands into the fly of my pants, and tens of men shoving each other in order to get to us. I still imagined that my response and screams of "Stop, you animal!" would make some kind of difference. I kept screaming, "Stop, you animals!" like an idiot, even though I knew that screaming wouldn't do anything. The idea that a scandal will make people gather and help—an idea I was used to on the street in an everyday sense— was useless here. I was hitting and pushing and screaming, but the truth of the matter was that the harassers weren't afraid of a scandal because they were so many, and everyone saw everyone harassing. Either someone joined or he wasn't able to do anything.

My friend and I were squashed between the people and the *foul* cart (she was carrying the bag on her back and I was holding tightly on to the straps of the bag). She held onto me by my shoulders tightly and said calmly and reassuringly (unfortunately, this experience had happened to her before and her understanding of the situation was far calmer and better than mine), "We are being attacked right now and the most important thing is that we stay together, no matter what happens." Nothing else mattered to her other than reassuring me, and she kept saying, "We're going to get out of this, we're going to get out of this, don't be scared, we're together." She kept repeating, "We're together, don't separate us," again and again. I held onto her tightly and felt all the hands groping every part of my body. After that I didn't feel anything other than that they were pushing me. In the midst of the terrible numbers and the horrible shoving, we moved away from the *foul* cart (that had been protecting our backs). Suddenly we were in the middle of the street, and the five pairs of hands became many more. They were grabbing me everywhere on my body and trying to put their fingers in my behind over my pants and in the fly of my pants with the utmost violence and savagery.

I felt something pointed and became really afraid. I realized one of them had something pointy and small and was trying to insert it or use it to cut my pants. I was screaming and really choking and crying, I couldn't do anything. I kept screaming hysterically, I kept screaming, "Shame on you! Shame on you!" for a very long time, I don't know why. I couldn't see my friend at all. They were pulling the scarf around my neck and choking me and dragging me by it (the worst thing is for someone to be wearing a scarf around their neck in the clashes) and I was choking, I couldn't breathe … I forgot all of the advice that I had learned in our group. I forgot that I needed to stay calm and that my screaming attracted them even more. The more I screamed the more savagely they attacked me. Right in front of me, I saw someone (I remember the way he looked: less than twenty years old and short and with the utmost savagery) cutting my sweater and cutting my bra and stripping it off of me. He kept grabbing my breasts and at the same time people were violating my body everywhere. I was so disgusted and felt sick. I felt like I was going to pass out. I was really scared I was going to fall to the ground. The shoving and the hands multiplied, and suddenly I stopped screaming, I couldn't breathe and I got really dizzy, and I was afraid I was going to fall down and die, I really felt that death wasn't far at all.

The pushing and the crowding was unbelievable, and I kept saying to the boy that was grabbing my breasts that I was dying and I kept trying to convince him that I couldn't breathe and I was going to die. In the midst of all that shoving my sweater had reached my neck and my chest was completely naked. Everyone around me was grabbing my breasts and one of them was trying to undo my belt and pull my pants off my body, so there would be a place for someone else to stick his hand. He stuck his hands in my pants and kept scratching me with his fingers, grabbing me really hard and hugging me and screaming, "Leave her alone, you shitheads, leave her alone!" While he was screaming, he was sticking all his fingers inside my pants, and so many of them were grabbing my breasts and so many people were pushing. Belts were hitting everyone everywhere. I felt like I was going to throw up and I was really dizzy. I don't know how much time passed and how people shoved us until we arrived at a corner in the wall next to Pizza Hut. We protected our backs with the wall, and a man kept hitting anyone around us and saying, "Shame on you, she's about to die," and kept screaming, "She's going to die because of you." Suddenly flames ignited from a hairspray can in front of me and the crowd dispersed, like insects. There were just two harassers left, stuck to us, continuing the assault. I saw my friend next to me again. The filthiest creature was the one who was grabbing me everywhere on my body, screaming as if he were defending me, while in reality it was his hands inside my pants. He was screaming, "Leave her alone, leave her alone!" All my attention was focused on him not undoing my belt and at the same time there were two men standing next to me completely calmly, grabbing my behind. They ignited more hairspray and suddenly there was a corridor for us to run into Pizza Hut. People pushed us inside and the rest of the harassers tried to enter and attack people who were standing outside, they were screaming and banging on the door. They closed the outer metal door of the shop completely and gave me a sweater. My friend's head was covered in blood.

I swear that what happened to me is just a quarter of what has happened to many other girls.

The attempt to terrorize us will not succeed, our anger and determination have doubled. I am truly sorry for all the girls who have experienced anything like this, I promise we will not be silent.

September 2012

I first met Farida at Nahya's house, in the kind of bright, energetic scene that became painful to remember when we were coming to terms with the revolution being past.

It was a couple of months before the attacks began. Nahya had invited a lot of people, maybe thirty or so, to her small apartment in Heliopolis.

I arrived on the earlier side and Farida was there already, sitting on the floor handling a camera lens. There are people, I think, who have more electricity than the rest of us and this is what I remember, that she seemed like she was moving even when she was totally still. She was wearing a white shirt and beige trousers with a big belt, chunky shoes, an enormous pile of black hair at the top of her head.

She smiled at me, introduced herself, and tried to place me.

"Are you with Mosireen?" she asked. Mosireen is a collective that worked to compile, film, and publish videos about revolutionary action and confrontation, countering the narratives given by security forces and the state. Many Opantish organizers were part of the collective.

"No, I'm just friends with a bunch of them. I've known Nahya for ages. You?"

"Yep," she said. "I knocked on the door and one of them answered and was like, 'We're in a meeting,' all rude, and then closed it in my face. So I banged on the door again and when he opened it, I said, 'I know how to edit with Final Cut. I can do twenty hours a week. I sent you an email, you told me to come.' "

Immediately, I understood that she was a person without any affectation. There was a lot of posturing around the revolution but something in Farida was always direct, independent, un-jargoned. I liked her right away.

Reading her testimony for the first time, I had to get up from my chair more than once, as if to get some distance from it.

belts hitting everyone everywhere
something small and pointy

It was the same when I read it again years later, working on this book.

choking me with my scarf, I was sure I was going to die

Like many survivors, she ended her testimony with a promise: *I promise you we will not be silent.*

5

January 30, 2013

Opantish Mission statement:

The idea that women's clothes or their presence in certain places are the reason they are sexually assaulted is itself a kind of punishment to victims. Group sexual assaults are organized acts that try to affect women's participation in the public field and especially the squares, sit-ins and mass protests.

At the first meeting for new volunteers after the anniversary attacks, people were spilling out of the conference room and into the hallway. We were in the offices of a human rights organization where a couple of the organizers worked and where small groups had had some of the earliest discussions back in the fall, before Opantish had a name or an identity. Now organizers rushed to move furniture to the back of the room to make space, and they asked people to sit on the floor.

Once everyone settled, T stood at the front of the room and spoke into a wireless mic. "We get asked a lot about whether women should be in intervention groups," she said. "The truth is that each person should look very clearly at the risks of any role that they take on. That goes for men just as much as women.

"While I was helping a woman, trying to get her out of a mob assault, we were separated from everyone else in the team," she started. "I was assaulted myself. There is no shame in what happened to me or in what happened to her."

Her voice picked up force. She had no tics, made no movements as she spoke. She held the mic with one hand and kept the other in her pocket. Her eyes—a remarkable gray—were steady as they moved around the room.

A young man sitting in the middle of the room raised his hand but didn't wait for her to acknowledge him before he spoke. "But isn't the truth that women are a liability—it's not only that they become targets themselves, but also they don't know how to fight, they can't help the group in confronting these men ..."

He was cut off not by T, but by Nahya.

"I'm going to stop you here," Nahya said. "This group is about women, and as you can see it's mostly organized by women. This isn't about men coming in and saving women, saving their bodies or their honor." Her eyes have lit up with anger, and she seemed to grow taller as she spoke.

"We are a feminist group, we've always made that clear," she continued. "So we will never, ever tell women that there is something they cannot do in this group, and if you or anyone else has a problem with this, you really should just leave."

The man didn't respond, and he didn't leave.

T took the mic back from Nahya.

"The other night, I learned something important that I had not really understood until I saw it. Many times, women under attack are in shock, and this can look very different in each case: they can be panicking, they can be catatonic and completely disconnected. They can't trust men who say they are there to help them—it doesn't matter what T-shirt they are wearing or what group they say they belong to. They can only trust a woman, they can only start coming back to themselves when they see other women or hear a woman's voice. So when we insist on having women as part of our intervention, it's not just about feminist principles: it's also about practicality."

Several women in the room nodded in agreement.

As we split into specialized teams, a tall, pale woman came up to me. She introduced herself and asked, "Where do you think I should go?"

"Is it your first time?" I asked.

"Yes," she said. "I wanted to join before but I wasn't really ready."

I nodded.

"Do you think it's safe for women to go with the intervention teams?" she asked.

"There are different risks with each role," I said. I tried to be exact with my words. "Would it help if you talked with someone who's been on intervention before—a woman?"

"You haven't been on intervention?"

"No, I haven't. Really, there's a lot of other work to be done."

"OK, well, maybe I'll join the safety teams," she said.

"I've been on safety before," I offered. "It's not as dangerous as intervention, but there are still some risks. You might get separated from your partner, and find yourself alone. You might get harassed or become targeted. I don't mean to discourage you ..."

"That's OK." She looked me in the eye. "I'm so glad to be able to do something. I think if I had to hear about this happening one more time, and there was nothing I could do about it, I'd go crazy."

"I know what you mean," I said.

In a separate room, Seif and Leila led a meeting with the intervention teams. There were about fifty people there, about two-thirds men.

Leila could sense the women in the room watching her. Most of them were new and didn't seem to know one another. She knew what they saw: an activist type with bags under her eyes, dressed in worn leather boots and the olive-green jacket she'd been wearing in cooler months since the revolution began. Her hair was short, her nails bitten down and scraggly, and she wore no makeup. Some of the other women shared this look, but others were much more coiffed. One woman, in heels and a pantsuit, looked like she'd come straight from an investment bank.

A woman sitting near the back asked "Is there a system for trying to identify these men? Is it possible that some of them are repeatedly attacking women, I mean that they're there over and over again?"

"We don't have a system, but of course we talk between us when we debrief," Leila said. "But the mobs are so chaotic that a lot of the time it's impossible to tell who is doing what—people are attacking, are stealing, are filming, are there just fighting, and others are actually trying to help. This is why we decided early on *not* to try and identify or punish attackers. I personally don't think it's possible, and I think it would drag on and escalate the fighting when what we want to do is to get out of there as fast as possible. Our focus is on the *woman*."

A young, clean-cut guy she'd never seen before raised his hand. "I heard there were guns that were pulled on people," he said.

"There was one, yes. Some kid from the Black Bloc group threatened someone with it. But there has never been a gun on our side."

"So what kind of weapons will we carry?"

There was an edge of excitement in his voice. Leila tried not to roll her eyes.

"After what happened on the 25th, we can't stop people from carrying tools to defend themselves. Some people carry American sticks (batons with a hidden switch blade), others carry electric tasers, others don't carry anything. But the most dangerous thing one of us could do is to carry a weapon that we don't know how to use," she says.

A guy in the front row typed something into his phone, and Leila realized they should have asked people to leave their phones at the door. One recording of this kind of talk could land them all in military court.

Down the hall from the intervention teams, in a small conference room with a big glass window onto the corridor, the safety team volunteers gathered. T and Eman were in the lead. The atmosphere was nervous, almost tense. It was known that this was the team where a lot of women were assaulted, that others had been stranded, and that the team generally hadn't been able to do its job.

But T and Eman had a plan. They didn't know each other very well, but right away there was a clear respect between them. They wanted the team to be safe and efficient but, even more important, they wanted it to be able to work without direction from the core group.

When Eman lived in Dubai, where she'd worked as a corporate marketing expert and used her vacation time to backpack around the world, she'd said she would only move back to Cairo to work on sexual harassment. At the time of this meeting, she was living in her parents' house in a faraway suburb because she hadn't had time to find an apartment. Since she spent all her time in the center of the city, the trunk of her car was a sort of wardrobe: toiletries, spare clothes, a pair of salsa dancing shoes.

As she spoke, Eman used a whiteboard to draw a circular map of Tahrir with Xs marking where intervention teams and getaway cars would be stationed.

"So what we've learned," she said, "is that the safety teams that carry the backpacks with the extra clothes—you guys—shouldn't actually be moving within the intervention teams. It's just too risky, the safety unit almost always ends up either getting dragged into the fight or completely separated from the team."

Eman herself was attacked in November while carrying a safety kit on her back, but she didn't share this.

"The getaway car system also wasn't working," she said. "We had one driver per car, and they usually weren't able to navigate the crowds or figure out the fastest routes on their own, on top of communicating with the operations room and the intervention teams. Plus, most of the drivers were men, and women didn't want to get into the cars with them."

She tried not to speak too quickly. There was a lot to get through, and she wanted to make sure she was understood.

"So from now on we'll put two people in each car: one to drive and the other to communicate with the rest of the group. And this second person's job is ultimately to care for the women who come to the car. The driver can be a man or a woman, but this second person *has* to be a woman."

A woman raised her hand and asked, "Is there any training on how to behave with women, with survivors, in situations like this?"

"Yes, this is very important," T said. "There are some basics that we're going to go over, about how to deal with survivors, how to be sensitive and not retraumatize someone. This isn't just for new people—I think it's useful for everyone to think about this, because we get caught up in what we're doing and sometimes we forget."

When the meetings end, I make copies of the signup sheets for each team and sit at someone's computer to type them up and email them to the organizing group. I sign myself up for the safety team again, although I know I'll also be involved in setting up the operations room.

Between the different sign-up sheets, there are more than two hundred names in total.

6

February 8, 2013

Yasmine El-Baramawy knew her appearance was part of this story, so she'd dressed casually, the way she might dress to go to a friend's house. She had no makeup on when she sat down at the long table in the TV studio.

Ten weeks had passed since it had happened, in November. Nadia was supposed to be with her, sitting next to her at the long table, under the hot and glaring lights.

Yasmine had known she wouldn't come even before she said, "I can't. My son."

She couldn't blame her, although she'd hoped for a togetherness with her in this, the way they had been together in so much else.

She'd had to tell her family she was going on television. She wasn't sure how much they already knew, whether they had connected her to the anonymous testimony that was shared online. Her mother might have. "God does not give us more to carry than what we can bear," her mother had written to her. Nothing more.

"I'm going to go on TV tomorrow," she told them all by Facebook message. One to her mother, one to her father, and one to her brother. Three messages, three ticks, three timestamps telling her when they read them. One response: a phone call from her father, begging her not to.

She didn't blame them for the silence. What do people say about things like this?

So there she was, no Nadia, just her and the host and two guests, both women. She'd felt she had to, and that she wanted to, after what happened on the 25th. The nineteen cases. Nineteen others. She hadn't been able to watch the video that Arwa had made, although it was everywhere. They would probably show it as part of this program.

"Two minutes," a man with a headset said from behind the cameras. "Please make sure your cell phones are switched off."

She had already put hers on silent. She left the text message from her father unopened. She imagined it would say: "What will the rest of the family think?"

She would make sure her voice was steady when she spoke. She would not show defeat or self-pity. She would not show anger. That was up to them—the people watching. She would move her feelings out of the way, out of the lights, so that there was space for theirs to grow in all of the homes where they watched her. She would be calm so that they could see her as one of them. Someone whole.

They will be furious, she thought.

"Fifty minutes?" the host asks. "The attack went on for fifty minutes?"

He is shocked without being incredulous. He believes her. The other guest—a women's rights advocate—puts her head in her hands.

Yasmine describes being carried by the mob from one neighborhood to another, being mauled the whole time. She was separated from her friend at the beginning, and at the end her only, final focus was keeping her jeans on.

The host's hand is on his mouth.

He says, "I understand you brought some of the clothes ..."

"The clothes I was wearing, yes."

She puts a plastic bag on the table.

"This is the shirt." It's red. Strips of dark red.

"And these are the jeans." She lifts them up.

The woman across from her still has her head in her hands.

"Those are ... those are cuts with a knife," he says.

"Yes," Yasmine says. Calmly.

Afterward, sitting in her car in the parking lot outside the studio, she lit a cigarette and looked at her phone. Over a hundred notifications.

There were two new messages from her father. She read them before she read the one he sent earlier, before they started filming.

"I watched it at the Ahwa. Everyone said you were tough and brave."

And later:

"Your Uncle Mamdouh called. He said to me: Your daughter is a hero."

7

At T's house, several intervention team organizers met to come up with a new strategy. A flip chart stood at the front of the living room, and the floor was covered in big sheets of paper ripped off of it, some scrunched up, some still lying flat.

Seif had started them off with some videos of clashes between protesters and police. Some of the footage was his own—he worked as a video journalist and often filmed labor strikes and mass protests. What they were focusing on was the way that the riot police moved into crowds.

He'd made sure Marwan was there too, thinking he might share something useful from his conscription, offer something about the way that military units move together. That was the goal: to come up with a strict, uniform formation for the intervention, a strategic plan of how each team could assemble and move itself in and out of the circles of attack.

Numbers were assigned for each position. Team members became not Heba or Ahmed but "4" or "2."

Seif drew it out on the big sheet of paper as best as he could.

"I wish we had a whiteboard," Peter said. "Also, your hand-writing is terrible." He was one of the younger guys on the team, who had been part of the early groups scouting for attacks, before Opantish existed. "Well, the numbers are what you really need to know," Seif replied.

Each intervention team would be at least twenty people strong —they had enough volunteers for that now. The teams would move through the midan in block formations, four people in a row, five rows deep.

When they were entering a mob, two columns of volunteers would go in first. The people at the front were expected to do most of the fighting and would use flares to scatter the crowd. Once they'd reached the woman under attack, they would shout out a code command, and those behind them would stand in two parallel lines, with their arms linked, each facing the crowd, forming a corridor out of the circle with their bodies. Ideally, they would not have to fight, they would just have to stand their ground, creating a safe passage between the center of the circle and its edges.

Once the corridor was formed, three or four women volunteers would go in to reach the woman and make a circle around her, facing inward toward her. More people would make a circle around them, facing outward and protecting this nucleus of safety. The concentric circles would move back out through the same safe corridor.

They were strategic about where to place the core of returning volunteers, depending on their levels of comfort with physical confrontation, which was often surprising.

Interview

Bahaa, 2015: "I'm not a fighter myself, but I remember being very skeptical at first about M as one of the internationals in the intervention teams. There was this xenophobia in the square by that

point—people accusing foreigners of being spies and all that—
and I thought that having M with us, who was this tall, blonde
white guy, was a huge risk. He stuck out and I thought his presence might do more harm than good.

"I was so wrong. M was really confident and fast, throwing
barricades out of the way, moving us forward. Like a superhero.
You really never know what someone else is capable of in situations like that."

8

February 2013

Lina's feet moved, one in front of the other, but her heart felt huge as it pounded against her chest.

They came to a stop. She took a deep breath and pulled her hood up to cover her hair so that no one would grab it, and also, maybe, it would help her look like a boy.

There were men on the outer circle holding up their phones, filming, and the circles to the inside of them were packed, dark. She could not see except for one person ahead of her at a time. Next to one of the camera-holding guys, she stood on her toes to look in, but she could not see what he was filming.

She went over the formation in her head. Peter will light the flare and he and numbers one to four will fight their way in. She and her partner Sara will move with numbers five to eight, who will be in a circle around them, and behind them will be the rest.

Then numbers one to ten will make a corridor, standing with arms linked, facing each other, and the only people who will pass through will be her and Arwa and the girl or the woman or the women or the girls who are in the middle now.

She was still trying to remember where Leila and Peter would be, which numbers they were supposed to be, when Peter started yelling, "Make way! Make way!" and a long flame came roaring out of the flare his hands. Everyone started moving and she tried not to look backward, the movement stopped and she looked back one more time but all she could see was a stick raised, and she thought the arm raising it was wearing a white T-shirt. She could hear the zapping of electric tasers. They were moving faster now, it felt like the rings of people could go on forever, not a circle or a mob but an ocean of men. Someone in front of her started yelling, "Here! Here! Lina!" and she was being pulled forward, and she saw the woman. Someone in a white T-shirt was pulling her up from the ground. He was bending down, talking to the woman but she was shaking her head, she wouldn't look at him, she was just shaking her head and not speaking. Lina reached them and the teammate moved to the side so that she could face this woman.

"My name is Lina, I'm with Opantish, I'm here to help you," she said.

She had to repeat this twice, three times before the woman heard her but, when she did, she looked stunned for a second, and Lina wasn't sure if she was going to push her away. But then she threw her body into Lina's.

Lina tried to take off the backpack to take some clothes out, but the woman grasped her arm with both hands. Her grip was strong and over and over again she said *matsebeneesh*. Don't leave me.

Lina already knew that she was no longer a person who had come to help this woman. They were a unit now, and they would make it out together or not at all. Her other teammates were huddling around the two of them, to take them back out of the circle the same way that Lina had come in.

In our interview two years later, Lina tells me that after it was over and she had taken the woman home, she was shocked to hear that theirs had been the only attack that night.

9

Email threads from those weeks after the anniversary attacks link to news stories and online testimonies that are no longer just about the horror of the circles but about the people pulling each other out of them. Some of the stories are now about Opantish and the two other groups that were doing similar work, Tahrir Bodyguards and Basma.

Phone calls and online messages came in from around the country: from Alexandria, Damanhour, Minya.

"We want to make a group like yours. Can you give us any advice?"

"Do you have a chapter here in Tanta?"

"How do I join?"

"Thank you."

Leila forwarded a message from a woman she had pulled out of an attack. The woman had been stripped of her clothes in one of the circles but was now asking when the next meeting was so she could volunteer.

People sent money to us via intermediaries, asked where they could make a transfer to, or dropped cash off the few times we ran collection points at various cafes.

On a day that could have been any day in this story, when I was running some errand in the square wearing my Opantish T-shirt, a man I didn't know stopped me. He was young, in his thirties, wearing cheap office clothes that made me think he might have a job teaching or sitting behind a desk in a beat-up government office, an administrative position that paid modestly. Because I didn't know him and because he seemed very intent, my first reaction was to stiffen and take a step back. He looked me straight in the eye and started apologizing.

"I'm sorry, I don't mean to bother you, it's just that ... you're with the group? The anti-harassment group? I want to give you something ..." He reached into both of his pockets and brought up what was in them, parsed out the paper money and gave it to me. Everything he had.

I thanked him. He asked if he could volunteer, and I must have told him to follow us online or when the next meeting would be. I never saw him again.

We used the money we raised for the safety kits, the phones and phone lines, the T-shirts, and for hospital bills as they come up. Some of it went to weapons—flares, batons, tasers, American sticks. There were some experiments in protective gear, too. A few people tried out some chemical factory suits, like hazard suits, but they were too heavy and clunky to move in. One volunteer was inspired by the shields in the film *Troy* and had ten plastic prototypes made, only to be gently let down by the team captains, who found them impractical.

Tahrir Bodyguards and some of the other groups that did similar work to Opantish were much more geared up in terms of helmets, sticks, shields. Opantish went out in T-shirts, and volunteers concealed any weapons they carried until they needed them. In theory if not always in practice, we were going for de-escalation and to get out of the fight as quickly we could. We thought that going in flashing weapons and equipment around would encourage more fighting and not less, although that didn't always work.

Interviews

Bahaa, 2016: "Most men's first experience of violence against women is of being emasculated. Someone bothers or hurts your sister or your girlfriend but it becomes about you, the injury to your sense of masculinity."

Leila, 2018: "It took a very long time to convince people, to convince the men, to stop fighting, to leave once the women had got out. And in the beginning there were these terrifying conversations about weapons, where people wanted to bring serious things out with them, but we shut that down right away …"

Me: "Who shut it down? The women?"

Leila: "The women and the men, to be fair. The captains. There was one time when there was a gun, but actually this ended up working for our argument. It was a horrible attack, and it kept going on and on, and growing bigger and bigger, and most of us were stuck between the crowd and an iron fence, and we couldn't reach the woman. It was really terrible. And then this guy that I know from the Midan Security (many of whom we knew were with state security, and he was one of them) came in and he had a gun. He was on our side … anyway he fired a real shot in the air. And I was glad that he did, because it didn't do anything, it didn't stop the mob, it didn't help, and the volunteers saw that, and I think it helped us end this argument for good."

2017: When I get to Adam's place for our interview, he's sitting at his dining table building a birdcage. It's large, with copper bars that curve to meet at the top. Stepping in from the loud and busy streets below, I feel, for a moment, as though I've stumbled on a scene from a storybook.

(Years later, Adam tells me that the birdcage had been a decoy. He set it up on the balcony of the apartment, and in it was a real bird but also a concealed camera, which he used to photograph the street below as part of an art project. By then, taking photos on the street had become risky, attracting the suspicion of cops and honorable citizens alike.)

Adam is an artist with a talent for satire. He was part of the intervention teams and was close with Seif and Leila and Marwan. As we talk about the past, his eyes animate with genuine interest and curiosity. I sense that he's thought a lot about what happened.

A couple of hours into our interview, he mentions a microbus driver who had been on the team with him at some point in 2013. "I don't remember his name, he might not have been a driver, he might have been the guy who stands in the door of the microbus and yells out where it's going as it drives through." He wants to help me get in touch with this guy.

"He was a very nice guy with a very kind face. He saw us working one night and he was very moved. He said he wanted to join. He was a young man, not very social, probably no experience with women at all, and I felt that for him it was not only about stopping harassers, it was about much more. In some way, I felt that for him it was a way of getting involved with women, not in a bad way, not that he's profiteering, but it was a lead toward the other gender in the best way possible. And there are many of these."

Adam thinks Seif might know how to reach him, so we call him and he comes over. The three of us sit at the kitchen table, smoking cigarettes and drinking coffee. Adam puts some sweet potatoes in the oven.

Seif, who at some point was coordinating all of the intervention teams, still has the phone numbers of volunteers programmed into his phone. But they are not entered as names—rather, it is Opantish 1, Opantish 2, Opantish 3 …

"It was just easier," he says. "We had a list of who they were and their details, but that stuff all went to the database. Who did I give the lists to?"

He goes through them to see who is on WhatsApp and if they have photos of themselves up.

"No, that's not him. This guy was younger."

He sends a message to a couple of them: "Hi, how are you?"

A photo of Opantish 16 comes up, and I recognize him as someone who went to university with me whose name I can't remember. But I'm sure it was him, a bro-ey, loud, elite type.

How would he and the microbus driver have dealt with each other? How much was class already informing my and Adam's guess about the reason for the driver's involvement with Opantish? That it somehow would blow his mind open? That upper-class men have more varied interactions with women, that this somehow means that they have a better way of dealing with gender?

2017: A week after my interview with Adam, Seif comes over to my apartment. When he walks in, he looks stunned for a moment and stands still in the hallway, like he is surprised by where he is or was expecting something different to open up before him.

We sit in the kitchen, and I make him coffee in the little red mocha pot I've just bought, a small domestic act that helps me feel settled as my life moves between two cities.

"Is this a smoking-friendly room?" he asks. I say of course and point to the ashtray on the table.

"Now I remember the last time I saw you in a house, like this, away from the madness. It was when you were living downtown, right? And we all came over for a meeting or for dinner? The Opantish crew?"

I remember that before Seif arrived, someone had draped a black shawl over the liquor that was on a table to the side of the room. He was struggling with a relapse around then; it got worse after the coup.

He says he's clean now and working with an independent media production company. I think about the overlapping arcs of his life, what a cluttered graph they would make: the revolution's ups and downs, the climax of Opantish and the coup, so close together, his own battle with addiction in crests and dips throughout.

He says he is sure he was already traumatized way before Opantish existed, from the violence against the revolution. I want to press him for more but I feel I shouldn't just now.

Seif talks about the transformations he thinks have stuck with men from their experiences with Opantish.

"The real impact Opantish had on men was in changing this perception of 'what a woman is.' It went beyond the assaults ... there was a lot of quiet time, times when we'd go out and nothing would happen. People would talk, they'd hear things, interact. They remember realizing the importance of the debate around whether to use the words "victim" or "survivor," the tips about how to behave with women who had been attacked. It showed them how to be sensitive and caring, how to do no harm. They remember very clearly how this changed them, what it taught them, and they're proud of it."

He felt his role was to show up and follow decisions made by the female organizers. "All of my experiences of harassment or oppression of women in general have been through the women in my life … so with Opantish, I felt my role was just to be there. This was their resistance."

10

Adam drew in strength when he looked at the rows of white T-shirts around him. In his team, Team 3, there were twenty-three other people. There were three other teams positioned at different points around the square. They were standing in rows of four, a formation that Seif had built into the plan. He had listened closely as Seif and the other team captains had gone over it.

They got the signal and started moving to the corner of Mohamed Mahmoud. Adam was in the second row. Movement was easier than before, when they were following one another in a random herd, looking over their shoulders to make sure no one had been grabbed along the way. Now they pressed forward, trusting that everyone would play their part.

He could feel in his heartbeat how this made him stronger, more confident. As they walked, people made way for them to pass through. They were a block of white, and everyone knew who they were and what they were doing.

He couldn't see past the shoulders in front of him but when he heard Seif shout "TWO!" he knew they'd arrived. There was shouting and pushing and within a few seconds he heard the roar of the flare and suddenly everything around him was black. There were no faces to make out, but the shouting continued.

"YOU FAGGOT YOU PIMP I'LL KILL YOU AND I'LL KILL YOUR MOTHER."

These men could be anyone.

"NOT LIKE THIS, DON'T BEHAVE LIKE THIS, YOU'LL KILL HER IN THERE."

They could be anyone at all.

"GET OUT OF HERE. ARE YOU HER FATHER? IF NOT THEN GET THE FUCK OUT OF HERE!"

Even if he saw their faces he knew he would never recognize them again.

"I'M HERE TO GET HER AND I'LL DIE AND KILL YOU BEFORE I LEAVE."

Adam had another plan, one that he'd agreed to with some of the others. He felt ready, and even if he wasn't he had to be because for the woman in the middle every second was a hell, every heartbeat a new nightmare that she had to get through. She was real. The rest was theater: the men clawing at each other, screaming lies about who they were and why they were here. They were live, they were rolling. But she was real. And this was happening to her.

The men were within his reach now, these individuals who had become part of a whole that undefined them. Adam picked the one closest to him, a man of thirty or so who had a belt raised in the air.

He was close enough now, and Adam leaned toward him and said, very quietly, "We're here to help. I know that you're here to help, too, *of course*."

The man's head jerked backward, as though he had been sprayed with cold water.

"I know you're trying to help that poor girl."

The man turned to look at Adam, and for a second there was

anger in his eyes but then there was something else. It wasn't sympathy, but it wasn't anger. It was a kind of pain.

So Adam said, "We need to work together to end this and save this poor girl."

The man looked at Adam, looked down at his T-shirt, said, "There are more of you?"

"Look, there's a whole team of us. We're here to help you save her," Adam replied.

The man nodded. He spoke more quietly now. "Yes, yes, yes, of course, that's what we're doing, we're here to help."

"I was sure of this."

Of course.

"Hold this guy's hand so you can help us make a corridor," Adam told him, nodding toward another volunteer and making his voice a little more energetic, a little more excited, but without making it louder. As though this was now a pact between the two of them.

Using his wrist, the man looped the belt he had been holding into a tight coil and put it in his pocket. He put his right hand in a volunteer's and Adam stepped back as he shouted: "Make a corridor, come on, your hand in mine."

He could see that one of his teammates, Nada, was leaning in to speak to someone, and it looked like she was whispering in his ear.

He felt a flash of fear for her. But the seconds, the heartbeats were ticking by.

The corridor was forming in patches. He looked for the next person to talk to.

Interview, 2017

Me: "Do you remember when you figured this out?"

Adam: "We always knew that people could be either/or."

Me: "Because women themselves had said that people sometimes switched during the attacks?"

Adam: "People just go crazy, they're encouraged by the others. But they could also want to be good people, with another social status. Do you want to be a harasser or do you want to be a hero? So we encouraged them to be heroes, by speaking with them very calmly, very intimately, speaking in their ear. Never adding to the sense of danger and hysteria by shouting or creating panic. We aimed to be a very quiet force, to allow people to come back to their senses in very small touches."

Me: "Did you find that difficult to do, to stay a peaceful presence?"

Adam: "You do it at a price, of course, because inside you're boiling and you're afraid. But you can only diffuse madness and hysteria by being the exact opposite. It becomes almost weird, like who is this block of ice in this fire, you know? It's the contrast that has effect."

Me: "It's like a performance."

Adam: "Yes, completely. It's an act."

Me: "Except you're on the most terrifying stage."

Adam: "It's like whispering into someone's ear at a death metal concert and talking to them about Plato."

11

Not everyone is as positive about the men in Opantish as Seif and Adam's stories suggest. I hear from several people about the inflated egos and the personal credit that men gained from their participation in ways that women did not. Adulation poured out for them on social media and when they spoke on television; gendered ideas around bravery and heroism persisted, and some men used this for social or sexual gain. One organizer tells me she dated a man who asked her, "Opantish, isn't that the group that men joined to pick up women?"

Interviews

Marwan, 2016: "The problem with Opantish was that it gave a feeling—on the day itself—of personal victory: you're a good person, you went out and prevented these assaults or helped these people. That's all great. But the problem with the feeling of victory is that it makes people uncritical about deeper things in their lives with women that don't have these vulgar scenes of harassment. You feel like you're a good person—but that's not necessarily true. Just because you're not like the harassers doesn't mean you're all good toward women. I've seen friends, and maybe myself, where we'd go out with Opantish but it wasn't translated into rethinking our relationships with women, for example.

"Women are people who can't move in the street, so of course this is their fight. But men get a certain privilege by being there. They're seen as being 'good'."

Men did not post or share testimonies of the harassment that they experienced in the course of this work. Several mentioned being fingered or otherwise sexually assaulted; Omar told me about going out to buy the tightest pair of underwear he could find and wearing it in layers before going out. But in the same breath, they maintained that these injuries were minor next to what was done to women. They consistently dismissed the injuries to their own bodies, sexual or otherwise, the way that women so often do: *what happened to me wasn't as bad as what happened to the others; it wasn't rape; I was lucky.*

Omar, 2015: "Your involvement is based on this gender-based guilt and it's a relief to just be told what to do in that scenario. Not just because you're a man and it's men doing this but also because you haven't been doing anything about any kind of gender issue ever before. We had that moment after 2011 when no women were elected in the parliamentary elections and we all said that this wasn't the time to divide demands and that we needed to be united, and I just went along with that because that was the discourse coming out from the women around me, who were the people I took political cues from anyway. But then when this started happening, you feel complicit for being a man and for not having done anything about anything before."

Me: "I remember seeing you at Stella bar or something and you talking about that, about feeling guilty, and you even looked kind of guilty. I remember the look on your face, you looked upset."

Omar: "It was so horrifying that it was the end—in one stroke —of anything that was left of the innocent optimism. I remember thinking: how do you do anything after this? How can you have any interest in humankind or human society after this? How do you carry on having any kind of political idea about what you're doing? It was politically devastating. Having a mindless foot soldier role is kind of useful then. You don't have to ask any questions about what you're doing or why, there's no question about why."

12

Interviews

TV shows wanted to do segments, some wanted to film us during operations, although we never agreed to that because it would have interfered with the work. Reporters wrote stories for both domestic and international papers, and while they often asked whether the attacks were premeditated, the violence was also linked to Egypt's endemic problems with sexual harassment.

Muslim Brotherhood members tweeted that violence like this didn't take place at their own rallies. A police general who sat on the human rights committee of the upper house of parliament said women were "100 percent" responsible for being assaulted. What brought them out to the square in the first place?

T, radio interview, 2013: "We believe a big part of the assaults is organized. Sexual violence was always used as a tactic by the system to punish women who take part in protests … The system is the same system, the system has not changed yet, all that's changed is the head. We've had similar cases during the past two years, and even during 2005 … We're being attacked for being women. This is part of the struggle and this is a very personal fight."

(In 2005, on what came to be called Black Wednesday, police kettled a peaceful demonstration, and men in civilian clothes—hired by the ruling party and its security forces—assaulted, stripped, and beat the women protesters.)

T, 2016: "When I read our statements from back then, it's comical, it's embarrassing. At the beginning, our line was that this was premeditated, by the end we were like, no, we have a bigger problem. Even if it's preorganized, the state might send a hundred people, but there are two thousand others in the street ready to take part in a rape. And that's the real problem here.

"There were moments of mass hysteria ... I saw belts cutting people's faces open, but they just kept going, like zombies. Even the natural human reaction of self-preservation is not there."

Me: "I've heard explanations that we're all influenced by energies coming from each other and from what's around ... so maybe in a mob it becomes so saturated and hypnotizing ..."

T: "But it's very strange that this hypnosis happens only to men." (Laughs.)

There are still no answers. As T said, some of us thought the attacks were premeditated. But as time went by, an unsettling feeling that they might not be, or that they might have been but were no longer, or that the violence was only partially orchestrated, was forcing us to confront the reality that at least some of the people doing this harm were people we might have stood shoulder to shoulder with at demonstrations or in battles with the police. People we otherwise considered allies, revolutionary comrades.

Marwan, 2016: "The thing is, Opantish threw out all the old explanations. It threw out the explanation that violence against women is the result of a chain of oppression. There is no stronger moment than the moment of revolution. People had broken from that chain of oppression, had broken it within themselves, and this was still happening.

"And the explanation that the state sent these people is too easy, it allows for denial. It creates this picture where there are always the clear bad guys. It's not true. I saw people who were with us on the same front line against the police, and they were harassing women."

(Pause.)

"I think it's from the heart of society."

13

February 2013

Yasmine knew better than to look at his eyes, but she couldn't help it.

"You fucking bitch," he said to her, and he wasn't shouting but his voice was raised.

It was a week after her TV interview. About ten of their friends were in the living room with them.

"Why are you doing this? You want your moment in front of the cameras so much that you're willing to make us all look bad? You want to shit on the revolution?"

They'd all been talking about music before the conversation turned to the interview.

She had gotten used to his face without eyes. Other people looked at him and his blindness was all they saw. He was the maimed hero of the revolution, his loss a badge of honor that made his words more compelling. First one eye was lost to a shotgun pellet in 2011. The other was lost the same way, months later.

But Yasmine lived with him and his wife. She knew him beyond his injuries.

Before she had agreed to go on television, she had asked him to speak up about the attacks, to write a post to his thousands of followers.

"Why should I believe you?" he asked her. "I can't talk about something that I've seen no evidence of."

She had no wound to show, no absence.

"You're just not pissed off about it," she said to him.

"What do you want me to do about it?" he said over and over.

Part II

When am I a victim, and when am I a survivor?

—T, 2016

More and more I began to link these intense attacks which have clear objectification of women's bodies with everything else that has nothing to do with Tahrir ... with [female genital mutilation], with marital rape ... I linked all of these things together. To me it was just another manifestation of this horrible thing called patriarchy and domination and objectification of women and not feeling that women are humans and not thinking about their pains ... it was really clearly manifested in the attacks, but what's the difference between this and cutting your daughter's clitoris?

It's this brutal dealing with women's bodies and women, this huge alienation from them. It's in words like "I don't understand women, women are strange beings," these little words, this stuff is meant as a joke, but to me it's linked to what happened. It's in this huge distance from this thing that we can hold and grab and cut and play with and throw and hurt ... this horrible distance.

—Nahya, 2016

14

On the fourth day of being alone, T woke up just after noon. The sound of traffic came up through her windows and walls. The sleeping pill had worked—it always does—but now she was groggy and heavy. She needed coffee.

Before going into the kitchen she stopped at the apartment door and checked that it was locked. She turned the key to unlock it and then turned it back again, pushing the metal bolt through three times.

The first thing that went wrong was that the paper bag of ground coffee beans, bought from the roastery a few blocks down the street, was almost empty. There was only half a teaspoon in there. Fine. She would order a Nescafe and some other things she needed from the grocery store.

She picked up the telephone and realized she didn't know the number to dial. It was saved on her cell phone, which was in a dresser drawer, switched off. Before she'd put it away she'd sent a text message to Adam, to Nahya, and to her brother, saying that she would be off the grid for a while. She'd learned, from previous crashes, that this was better than unresponsiveness setting off the first alarm.

She rummaged through the packets of plastic cutlery on the kitchen counter, from so many food deliveries. Menus, tissues, receipts and, there in the back of a drawer, not the card with the name and phone number of the grocer but something better: a thin, individual packet of a new Nescafe 3-in-1: a Nesca-Mocha. Fine.

A frame flashed to her mind: Habiba unpacking a delivery while they were working on a press release. "Gross!" she'd said, holding out the purple and yellow packets of Nesca-Mocha for everyone to see, to agree with her indignation. "I asked for a jar of Nescafe Gold, man. This is vile."

T took the cup of instant coffee to the far end of the living room. The night before, when the anxiety had smoothed over enough that she could channel it into action, she had organized her canvases and drawing papers into piles on the coffee table, so that the drafts of specific drawings each had their own pile. Dozens of pens and pencils and brushes were in a row of jars lined up on the floor below them.

But this neatness, this compartmentalized orderliness, now irritated her. The room seemed empty without the explosion of papers and pens and tools on the floor, on the couches, the lines and colors of different scenes forming a crowd around her.

She started to wonder if she should call someone, maybe Adam. She lit a cigarette from a pack someone had left on the coffee table and thought about what she would say to him. "Come be with me but I don't know for how long"?

Or,

"Come have a coffee with me but you have to bring some coffee with you"?

Or,

"Come and see me but you have to be ready to leave as soon as I say that you need to go. No questions, no arguments"?

No, no. This wasn't the day for other people.

She looked at her drawings from the very beginning of the crash. The theme had been there from the start, the figures of faceless women, almost like outlines of a human being. Drawings of the borders of the body, no clothes, no expression, no details. Just the borders.

They are floating, in the beginning, just floating on the paper. Later, one figure is sitting in a bathtub. She is filled in with the color red. T didn't remember drawing this one. It made her sad. Alone, red, in the bathtub. Had she drawn this on the first day?

She took a sip of the Nesca-Mocha and began. Her hand moved over the paper, drawing more borders, with various shapes and sizes. Today was about scenes with multiple people.

The call to prayer came through a few hours later, riding over the traffic noises. She wished she could listen to music while she worked, but she couldn't focus. The voice of the muezzin calling people to prayer through loudspeakers at the nearby mosque was particularly grating—high-pitched and ugly.

She didn't notice the next call to prayer, at sunset. She kept going as the orange light seeped out of the room, kept going as it turned blue, only stopped to turn on the light when it was almost gone altogether. It began to feel as though, rather than trying to create something, she was taking something in.

Sometime later in the evening she heard the elevator stop at her floor, the heavy metal door open and swing back shut. Within a second, there were knocks on her door. She stopped moving and started counting in her head.

There was a pause on the other side, across the apartment, through her triple-locked door.

One, two, three, four.

She knew that the light from the lamp, next to her on the floor, would not flow out from under the apartment door. She had checked.

Five, six, seven, eight.

She had wondered if it would be safer, smarter, to block the space under the door with a towel to make sure nothing seeped through.

Nine, ten, eleven, twelve.

But what if whoever was on the other side crouched down, looked under the door, or slipped something underneath it and figured out she had blocked it? No, this way, there was less evidence that she was home.

Twenty-four counts in, another three knocks, and then, Adam's voice: "T, I just want to know if you're OK. Please."

One, two, three, four.

He didn't say anything more.

Eighteen counts after that, she heard the elevator door open.

She closed her eyes, thought of him going down the eleven stories in the fluorescent light of the elevator. How sad, how worried his face would look, how tired. She wondered if the cut on his forearm had healed. Had he had to get stitches in the end?

In the pause that she had taken from the drawing, waiting for Adam to leave, her brain had registered that her hand was over-exerted and was now sending her pain.

Fuck. Fine.

She rotated her wrist a few times, pulled at the fingers of her right hand with her left. She splayed the fingers out on the floor and stretched her palm back and forth. She looked at her nails, bitten down, uneven. She didn't remember biting them.

Another memory. It approached from far away, slowly.

She'd held her cell phone in her left hand as they were being squeezed out of the shop by the crowd. She had one arm wrapped around the shoulders of the woman in front of her, as they were finally making it out. She'd decided that it was safest to hold the phone in her other hand, because it would get taken straight out of her pocket and she could not risk getting stranded. In the sensory mess of the moment—the groping at her sides, the hands on her ass and in between her legs, the pulling on her jeans—she had felt someone trying to unwrap her fingers, one by one, from around the phone.

T looked down at the hands of the figures in the drawing in front of her. No fingers. She went through the papers lying on the floor from the day's earlier work, then the ones from the beginning of the crash. No fingers anywhere.

Fine. Better.

Her hand began moving on the page again. She kept going through the evening call to prayer, through the nighttime traffic noises, through the night, until she was spent and could feel, somewhere at the edges of herself, that sleep might come.

15

January 2015

Gray days are not quite gray in Cairo—they are white mixed with a very pale yellow, the color of the lightest straw wine. It is the coldest that the city ever looks, and it brings out a paleness in people's faces too, a drained-ness.

I've sublet my room in New York and come back here for the winter.

The noise is constant. Not just the blaring horns and revving engines of buses and the music from cars and shops at incredible volumes. There is also the noise calculated to convince us that we support our own oppression—nationalistic songs, dramatic ads against terrorism, statements about patriotic sacrifice on billboards and radio stations.

I feel both alienated from it but part of it, as though my skull and the membranes of my skin have become thin and open. No one is after me, but I still feel like there is nowhere to hide.

I'm in a taxi and Frank Ocean, in my headphones, battles with a radio presenter who is nearly shrieking as he insists that anyone who "shakes the faith of the people in the state should be eliminated." At the top of the hour a male and a female presenter alternate in reading the headlines; it takes six news items to get to one that is not centered around President Sisi, who led the coup that changed everything.

I look out the window and see women in various states of veil, walking in groups down the sidewalk. We are near Azhar University, where the walls are covered in black or white blots of paint, where the state's employees or its supporters have covered up graffiti pronouncing it corrupt, or memorializing January 25 or the Raba'a massacre, or the names of students killed and disappeared. It's too much to keep painting over each entire wall so now they just spray paint over the bits of graffiti and leave the rest.

I am on my way to visit my parents in Nasr City, the sprawling neighborhood where I lived for most of my university years. Extending westward from the autostrada that separates it from the older, colonially elegant Heliopolis, Nasr City was planned by the armed forces, who have large bases there: training camps, detention centers, recreational grounds, and hotels. They are each heavily fortified, often surrounded by concrete walls topped with barbed wire, bearing signs that warn against taking photos.

The neighborhood is built along a grid, wide, six-lane streets bisected by narrow pavements with traffic going in opposite directions on either side. Off each main road are smaller streets of residential buildings that were meant to be no higher than four stories but which in many cases grew to nine or ten stories thanks to building permits obtained by bribes or ignored altogether. The buildings block one another's light and jam the streets with parked cars. Every few blocks there is a park, some with children's swing sets and soccer pitches that come to life, others that are filled with trash.

Coming here always reminds me of the turbulence of my

adolescence and early adulthood, when I battled with my family for freedom to do as I pleased, to go out and come back when I wanted. They could not reconcile this with what they knew of how to be in this city, in a society that tells itself it is "naturally" conservative even if it can no longer do so with a straight face, because everyone knows that people have always done whatever they wanted to behind closed doors. As in so many other places, women's bodies are at the center of social control and public morality. I think I fully realized this in mid-adolescence, around age fifteen, when I started expecting my freedoms to progress in a way that was in step with what I had always been taught by my highly educated parents, especially by my mother: to be assertive and unafraid, to be responsible, to take care of myself and others. The realization that my sex meant that all of that would be made subservient to vague ideas of morality and respectability landed on me with dread. Dread and disappointment, because I could now see the limitations of the parents, the mother, whom I had always understood to be ambitious, independent.

Double lives are common among girls and young women in Cairo, who hide romances or party-going or whatever it is that they cannot negotiate with their parents or guardians. Since I could not have the independence I wanted, I turned inward and pushed everyone away, creating a space where I could live by my own hidden rules, a parallel life that appeared, from the outside, to fit within the bright red lines of acceptability. This space, from which I expelled my family, made it easier to lie about how I spent my time, where I went and with whom, and, eventually, what I wanted from life, what I thought about the world. I hid so many parts of myself from anyone who had any authority over me that hiding became a default behavior. I hid feelings from friends, hid opinions from teachers and peers, hid wants and hurts from lovers.

It was an exhausting and largely joyless way to spend a privileged youth, walled off inside myself and inside my own home.

Outside the house, the battle continued. Harassment is a problem everywhere in Cairo but this neighborhood, Nasr City, was where I experienced it most acutely, most consistently as a young woman.

Most days I would walk down the side street near our building and try to find a taxi to campus, which was downtown. If I couldn't, or if I was low on money, I would have to get the bus from Abbas al-Akkad, a monstrous, eight-lane artery rammed with traffic and commerce.

Side street harassment was lecherous stares or the occasional comment about my clothes or my hair or my breasts or, once, a group of men screaming obscenities out of their car's windows as they drove past. On Abbas al-Akkad, the stakes were higher. As I stood waiting for transport, men would slow their cars down and look at me inquisitively, asking in words or with their eyes if I would get in the car for money. More than once, drivers wanted me to see that they were jerking off.

Sometimes they would U-turn, coming up and then back down the road to pass me again. One occasion, a car passed me three times, the driver gesticulating more and more emphatically each time. I looked away, turned my back, walked up and down the sidewalk, feeling trapped in the open air. I remember wishing that the trees had thicker trunks so that I could hide behind them.

Years later, after I met Farida, I found out that her family lived in a big building on Abbas al-Akkad right where I would stand, waiting for the bus. One day when she was waiting for her own bus to her own university, a car wouldn't stop driving by her, the driver masturbating as he leered. Her anger grew into a rage so white-hot that it made her faint. She crashed into the sidewalk face-first, chipping three of her front teeth.

What effect do these experiences have on us? Maybe, even when we brush them off, they make us understand that our bodies are potential prey. I think I understood this from a very young age, at least from my first memory of a man leering at me. It was during basketball practice, and I was nine. My feeling about being watched, about the gestures he was making, which I didn't fully understand, was of discomfort. I don't remember feeling afraid—I don't think I was. I remember thinking about it afterward, at home, with curiosity.

My friend L recounts sensing that *something was going to happen* minutes before a man took his penis out as she was sitting on the sidewalk after school, eating ice cream with her best friend. "I remember feeling very sensitized, very aware that there was going to be some kind of communication here, something unusual, and I felt curious about what it was going to be. Before it happened, when the guy was just sort of around, my friend said we should leave, and I said no, let's stay. I wanted to know what was going to happen."

We don't always become activists, we don't necessarily talk about it. Still, these experiences shape how we understand our bodies, they impact the courses of our lives. It's often startling for me to walk down the street with a man, especially if he is tall. What ease, what comfort, to walk and have traffic be your only worry. Women are often taught they have reason to be afraid of the world—but what else does this threatened position bring out in us?

In the 2010s, I helped organize a literature festival in Palestine. Year after year we took artists and writers from the United States, United Kingdom, and other parts of the world on a bus through the occupation, its checkpoints and segregated roads, the political and military infrastructure of apartheid control more obvious in some cities and hidden in others. Always, Black and Indigenous guests read and understood this geography of power faster, more matter-of-factly than the rest. It's as though there's a network of sensory awareness that people who have to understand threat carry with them, a different way of reading the world.

16

Every once in a while, the internet lights up with stories and outrage and discussion about sexual violence against women. We talk about the importance of breaking the structures of silence that remain, of showing the world that this is a universal problem, that it is #everywoman. We say that it is important that we hear each other, that women feel heard.

Some of us say that it's not important to explain to men, that men already know. We remind one another that it's not up to the oppressed to explain her situation to the oppressor; we quote Audre Lorde on the exhaustion that this brings. Willful blindness is just that—it's not an absence of information that allows people to pretend that the problem is minimal or contained to exceptional circumstances. It's a refusal to acknowledge the whole package that enables this violence, because the package allows them certain privileges.

Rather than wondering about the efficacy of addressing men, can we think of breaking into their awareness as a by-product of us speaking to one another? Can we focus instead on our own networks, on thinking together, on resisting together, on supporting one another—openly?

While Opantish worked, it addressed the state as well as revolutionary and political groups who were not doing enough. But by insisting on working the way it did, it changed minds, even in its action-driven, not-enough-time-to-talk way. The change came from the work itself, from the way it was done.

Sexual violence in the Arab or Muslim world is often talked about as a cultural issue. To the world's imagination, Arab women most often appear as passive victims or exotic constructs. We blame the Arab female's suffering on the culture she is unfortunate enough to live in, as if that culture or religion is closer to some ancient script than it is to contemporary features of the international economy and media. White and Western feminism has historically been part of this problem, hitching a savior discourse to various imperialist and civilizing projects, including the invasion of Afghanistan in 2001. In reality, the systems of political, economic, and social control in Egypt are held up by—and hold up, in turn—the forces that run the prison industrial complex in the United States, that prosecute Europeans for saving migrants drowning off their shores.

Treating sexual violence as a problem of culture or class also makes it easily used against Arab societies and Arab men in particular. The attacks in Tahrir continue to be referenced as proof of the sexual deviance of Arab or Muslim men, a sort of fuel for a European obsession with feeling threatened by Muslims. Look, they say, this is what they do when they are let loose, when the police are not around, when accountability is lost in a crowd. This, they say, is their real culture, and it's what we must keep out of Europe, out of our cities, out of our playgrounds.

Interviews

M, 2019: "I don't like talking about Opantish with people in London or with people who weren't already very familiar with what happened. It just ends up sounding like you're showing off. You want to talk about it because it's this awful thing that happened, but people want to talk about how you did this great, heroic thing. And of course, I don't want to talk about it because of the whole "Arab men do bad shit" thing. Which is such a trope that, even if you point it out, your story still gets used in that way. I don't want to be this white person, this white trans woman, talking about how I saved brown women from bad shit that brown men did."

The tricky truth is that women do have a problem here, just as we have a problem in most places. It starts with gender boxes—girls do x, boys do y, and anything different is abnormal—and then is shaped by circumstance and by how much, and which, ground has been broken by feminists before us. By what those feminists ignored, out of necessity or out of choice, in the single-mindedness of each battle: for the vote, for equal pay, for the right to divorce, and so on.

We have a problem, in Egypt, protecting our bodies from abuse in public space. That goes for all bodies to various degrees depending on your social class, the neighborhood you live in, whether or not you are conscripted into the army. Women have a problem protecting ourselves from harassment. In the decade before the revolution, a lot of work was done by NGOs and rights advocates on sexual harassment on the street. There were awareness-raising campaigns, there was lobbying for better laws and law enforcement. Women wrote about it on the internet, helping others grasp a language for what we all experienced. There was a lot of theorizing about why harassment was so prevalent. People blamed economic conditions, general repression, chains of violence, simple impunity in a patriarchal society.

In 2012 and 2013, the problem spiraled into a horror that no one had thought was possible. Even now, it can be difficult to allow for the specificity of the circumstances of the mob attacks, when they also seemed to draw from such an ever-present violence.

Sherif, 2016: "How sexual were the attacks? It was deeply sadistic. Sadism in the sense that no one is deriving actual sexual pleasure … people are deriving social pleasure, some sort of hedonistic 'I did this' … let's say I'm an individual actor seizing on the moment … it's a means by which I can have *done* something, to express myself against a woman, against somebody who is alien to me, somebody who I find to be out of place or detestable, this othering. There's something about the way this had to be, it *had* to be to make the square unsafe for women, you presume it from the nature of the action not from the perpetrators. What was the overwhelming effect? Tahrir became a place that was dangerous. Of course we can talk about the domesticating impressions of women that we have, it fits in the sense that it contributes to the overall effect that it had. That their place is not here, that this isn't for you, and therefore that this is not a place where civilized discourse happens. And that's why the slogan 'A Midan Safe for All' was inspired, a way to phrase the question that hits the nail on the head … that it's a space that was safe for people's variegated expressions of who they wished to be and what they wished to have in their society."

17

April 2013

The party was on a terrace overlooking the Nile but it could have been for rich young people anywhere in the world—girls wore summer dresses, as if the streets surrounding us were different ones. Men held whiskey glasses or green bottles of beer. The atmosphere wasn't quite carefree but the soundtrack and the wardrobe were different from the run-down bars around Tahrir. Everyone was talking about their summer plans, joking about the electricity cuts, which were happening almost daily, and cursing the Brotherhood's government. I was talking to a friend's brother and trying to avoid discussing politics, but he insisted on it.

"I don't think the Brotherhood are equipped to govern," he said. "They're ruining the economy and causing irreparable damage."

I didn't want to argue with him because I didn't think it would be of any use. There was plenty to fault the Brotherhood for, and I thought we should fight for early elections. But right beneath his line about their incompetence I sensed a feeling beyond annoyance, an anger at Islamism and the poor and it wouldn't be long before we were talking about whether Egyptians were ready for democracy or if what we really needed was a strong leader and a decade of financing from the IMF.

"Forcing Morsi out of power would give the Brotherhood a legitimate grievance to hold on to forever," I said. "Also, it would mean military rule, at least for a while. I don't think generals should be in charge of the country, do you?"

His eyes dropped to my bare legs, and contempt took over his face. He was thinking that, were the Brotherhood really able to apply their vision of the world, I wouldn't have been able to dress like that, wouldn't have had the social enclaves within which to do so. He was probably also thinking that I shouldn't dress like that anyway, not without a boyfriend or fiancée nearby.

It's a look I'd seen from men before at parties and gatherings, which I felt was a response to the double betrayal that women "like me" were guilty of: betraying mainstream conventions as well as the codes of upper-class circles that think of themselves as socially liberal but also hold deeply paternalistic attitudes. "Why do you look so serious?" "Why is your hair not blow-dried straight, ever?" "Why do you ride taxis alone? Where is your car, your driver?" "Why don't you smile more?"

Later that night, another man asked me: "What personal rights are you missing here, in Egypt?" when I told him about the human rights organization I was interning with. I said something about women's rights, about freedom of expression, about gay rights. His face hardened, and then he actually asked me: "Do you have a boyfriend?"

There were no big rallies in the square in the spring of 2013, and in that quieter time some of us talked about how we could take female resistance beyond Tahrir, beyond protests. How we could turn it into a national movement. It seemed obvious. How else would the revolution continue? Women had been central from the beginning, and everyone had made a big deal of being surprised about that. Now it had become clear, been marked on our bodies, that the social is the political is the physical and there was no use in pretending otherwise.

"We could go to the universities, labor unions, and schools," Arwa said. "We should start chapters in towns and villages around the country."

In a notebook, I wrote: "Eventually we'll draw in the domestic sphere, and that's when we'll have real change: when the women who actually run most households in the country rise up against the husbands who beat and control and abuse them."

I made lists of people to talk to: leaders of past student movements, human rights advocates, radical organizers from the '70s, women in India and in Latin America who we should look up and learn from.

We talked about what Opantish could do outside of the square. For each suggestion put forward—patrolling public transport, for example—there was a reason not to act on it, usually along the lines of not wanting to become an NGO. This wasn't only because of compromising realities of funding and bureaucracy that NGOs have to navigate; it also came from an aversion to the way most rights focused NGOs dealt with sexual harassment. Many of them framed sexual violence as an issue of class, education, and awareness and called for tougher policing as a remedy.

For many of us, cooperating with the police or state authorities was out of the question. Aside from the long history of impunity around police abuse and torture of detainees, in the first year of revolution military police had forced protesters in detention to undergo so-called "virginity tests." Survivors, who were also beaten and abused in other ways, spoke out, and one young woman,

Samira Ibrahim, took her abusers to court. A high-ranking general told CNN the tests were done "because these women are not like your daughter or mine."

After the mobilization by Opantish, the spring months of 2013 felt politically suspended. There was a great deal of anger at the Brotherhood from revolutionary camps as well as wider society. Morsi had issued a constitutional declaration in which he exempted all executive decisions from judicial review, adding fuel to suspicions of the Brotherhood. There was also incendiary rhetoric from Brotherhood leaders, documented torture of opposition protesters by Brotherhood supporters, the betrayal of all the electoral promises and pacts they had made with revolutionary groups in order to keep the military's candidate from the winning the presidency in 2012, and a cavalier tone that seemed to define their approach to governance.

Meanwhile, the old military establishment had begun to gather political momentum, backstage at first. A public campaign called Rebellion appeared that spring and centered itself around a national petition against Morsi, demanding early elections or that he step down by June 30. We know now that that campaign was quickly infiltrated and controlled by military intelligence. The actual coup against Morsi would begin with large protests slated for June 30, but in reality its first steps were in motion throughout the spring. The government was failing, rebellion was everywhere. The only thing that was clear was that the square would be full, and Opantish had to be ready.

Part III

I was away the two weeks before June 30. I saw the emails between people in Mosireen, about going out to the marches and walking in twos, the fear about lists of people to be killed ... I thought everyone had lost their minds.

Then I came back on the 30th and went straight from the airport to Opantish. And as soon as I saw the streets, I knew. I knew that we (the revolution) had lost.

—Leila, 2018

Part III

18

June 30, 2013

10:00 p.m.

The long corridor on the other side of the accordion metal gate where T and Joanna stood at the entrance to the Tahrir metro station was completely dark. The gate was pulled most of the way shut but there was enough space for one person to get through.

"I'll go first," T said and squeezed in sideways through the opening.

"Go ahead, I'm right behind you," Joanna said, turning on the torchlight on her phone and beaming it ahead of them, and T felt a moment of gratitude that it was Joanna—maternal, middle-aged—who had come running down here with her.

T pushed aside her dread and tried to remember the layout of the station, which had been closed since the early weeks of the revolution.

The only information they had was what Adam had said in a hurry over the phone: that a young girl had been taken by a crowd to a police point in the station after an attack, that she was being pressured to undergo a virginity exam, and that the lawyers Opantish had called to intervene were still on their way.

They walked down the wide, dark corridor, Joanna's phone the only source of light. "I think——" T began but was interrupted by loud voices volleying off the walls of the corridor. She couldn't make out the words, but she was sure that the voices were male, that there were more than one, and that they were getting closer.

She recognized the pitch: these were joyous chorales of young men. There was repetition—a chant, sing-song.

"Joanna …," she started saying, but Joanna had already turned her phone's torchlight off.

"They're just partying," Joanna whispered. "Just stand still, maybe they'll pass us."

They pressed their backs against the wall. First they saw the light from the men's torch, bouncing around manically. The light was on the wall across from them, then it was on the ceiling, then it was to T's right. She could see its wide white beam going past Joanna: it landed on the wall a few feet beside her, and then it was moving again.

Now they heard their steps as well as their voices. Here they were—six or seven of them, and T finally could make out what they were singing: "Morsi's leaving and he's never coming back, back, back."

The singing was moving closer and closer, the light was bouncing around and then just like that the men walked past them, taking their song to the exit of the station, to join the crowds celebrating above ground.

When the singing had faded, Joanna switched her phone light back on. They kept walking into the darkness. T tried again to visualize a map of the station. Two lines ran through it. Four different directions. Four different platforms. Was there just one

central booth for tickets? Is that where the police office would be?
A wooden door to the side?

The corridor turned into an open space. The ticket booth sat
wide, the glass of its four windows reflecting only the empty darkness. Black and white printouts about ticket rates for senior citizens
were still taped on the inside. They walked on both sides of the
booth, shining the light on all the walls. There were no doors,
nothing that looked like a room or an office.

There were train platforms on either side of them. Joanna
pointed the light upward to the left: the sign read El Marg. To the
right, Helwan.

The silence was broken quickly, shockingly, by the rumble of
a train. It sped through the empty platform toward El Marg, the
cars lit up on the inside. The air around T and Joanna moved fast
and hot. Could the people on the train see them? What would
they see? Two women holding a light from a phone, wandering
around the dark.

"Let's try the other platform," T said once the silence returned.

They climbed over the turnstiles—Joanna shone the light for
T to go first, then she followed.

They walked down the platform. T could hear voices, muffled,
low. "Do you hear that?" she asked.

"Yes," Joanna said. Joanna's light moved carefully along the
wall as they walked. The blue and white tile stopped, and there
was a metal door, painted dark blue.

The light rested on the door handle.

T straightened her back.

She put her hand on the handle and paused for a second before
pushing it down. They were both surprised when it pushed right
open.

Inside the room, T and Joanna found a small wooden desk with a policeman in uniform sitting behind it. There was no plaque or namecard on the desk, no pictures on the walls.

A woman in her twenties sat on a folding table against the far wall. Another woman, wearing a dirty white doctor's coat, stood next to her.

"What's happening in here? Who is in charge?" Joanna said, looking around at everyone in the room.

"Everything will be fine," one of the uniformed men said. "This girl got into a bit of trouble, so we are making sure she and her mother are taken care of."

T noticed the mother for the first time. A slightly larger woman, she stood next to her daughter and shook her head, her eyes on the floor.

T turned to the officer. "We're taking them home. There are lawyers on the way. If you want to open a case file on this, you can deal with them when they get here."

The officer looked at her, tapping his fingers on the empty desk. She could feel the stares of the other men on her in the subterranean room.

Aboveground

Nahya felt so hot in the crush, but it was the multitude of bodies —of teammates—around her that made her able to act, to keep moving as her team made its way slowly through the packed square.

The noise was incessant, deafening. Vuvuzelas, drums, chants, people with loudspeakers opining, singing, rallying. She was unable to think. Green laser lights jumped all around them from within the crowd, from nearby buildings, from the numerous stages that had been set up around the square. On one stage, a police force musical band was getting ready to perform. They were at the entrances to the square, too, for the first time since the revolution broke out two and a half years ago.

Underground

"It's for her own good," the man behind the desk said. "She wants to do it."

"Yes, she needs to be reassured that she's still intact," said the alleged doctor.

Aboveground

Nayha's team passed a group of women chanting "Sisi, be my President!"

In 2011, General Sisi had said that the virginity tests forced on female protesters by military police were done to protect the army against possible allegations of rape.

Underground

"Get out of my way," T said and moved past the doctor.

T stood in front of the young woman. She recognized the catatonic look on her face.

"Do you want to leave?" she asked her.

The young woman looked at T but didn't speak.

Her mother said, "They told us it would help protect her rights, her honor. If anyone found out that she was violated ..."

Joanna cut in.

"Is this where you want your daughter to have her private parts checked? In a metro station, under the ground?" she asked her.

The woman didn't reply, but hesitation strained her face.

"If you want a full exam, we can take you to hospital with a proper doctor."

Just then the two young lawyers came into the room.

"Come on, let's go, let them deal with this. We will take you wherever you want to go," Joanna said.

This promise worked. The mother put her arm around her daughter and said, "Let's go," guiding her past the woman in the white coat.

"We're going, you have my number," T said to the lawyers.

The light from Joanna's phone guided them out of the station. T walked next to the young woman. Behind them, Joanna kept the mother engaged, reassuring her they know the way out. They climbed the stairs back above ground.

Military helicopters chopped circles above them, dropping flags down to the people packed below. Beamed onto the wide Mugamma building overlooking the square were the words THIS IS NOT A COUP.

19

January 25, 2015

During a long visit back to Cairo, I think I can slip back into my life here, but I find that life is gone. I see Nahya at a gathering the night after I arrive. She greets me with perfunctory kisses before going on to talk to someone else, as though we are just acquaintances. I am hurt but decide not to show it. Distance sets in. It will be a long time before I figure out that what is going on between us is simple: she is angry because I left. I am angry because she thinks leaving is easy.

I'd forgotten the way that Cairo's winter feels, how the cold gets into your bones, how you can't escape it, like a layer of unwanted skin. You are coldest when you are indoors—you pile on clothes and shawls and even socks, but still your bones ache with it. Your brain feels full of a flat, low static. I write: "My mind is in a vise." My handwriting gets smaller as the words continue and then stop abruptly. I don't bother to cross out the unfinished sentence.

Omar and I are on our way to buy groceries when we hear that a woman was shot dead by the police on her way into Tahrir. It had happened in the daylight, not far from his apartment. The woman was carrying flowers.

I don't know how to react. Two years ago there would have been people going to the hospital, to the morgue, in solidarity. Was anyone going now? I'm not even sure who to call and ask.

I'd tried to forget that it was the anniversary of the revolution. There are too many anniversaries to keep up with now, of victories and of massacres. Each one comes with fresh blood, puts new faces behind bars.

We stand outside the grocery store, reading the news on my phone. The woman's name was Shaimaa. She had short hair and a son, and she was a poet and a leftist. Her son's picture is already online. He looks about four years old. Who will tell him that his mother has died, and how she died? When will he watch the video of her being shot? Will the adults in his life hide it from him? For how long?

I can't go inside the shop. But I can't go home. The uselessness has turned me to stone.

After the coup, the new government banned protests: taking part in one can carry a five-year jail term. The day after Shaimaa's murder, there is a call for a women's protest demanding accountability for her death. Limiting the action to women might make it harder for them to brutalize and round everyone up. Instantly the Facebook page organizing the demonstration is flooded with criticism: so many have died, is her life more valuable because she was not veiled, was not with the Brotherhood, because this happened in downtown Cairo rather than a distant suburb?

There are sharp responses, including one from T: no one is stopping anyone from organizing for any of the victims. Tearing this down is not constructive. Go ahead and organize for whomever you think needs organizing for, but leave us to do our own.

A quiet voice in my head thinks, *It's true. They are not coming from a good place, but it's true. We only grieve for our own now. There is an us that is different from them, even if we are killed by the same guns.*

The day of the protest, I wake up and admit to Omar that I wish it were canceled. I want there to be some emergency, something to take away this cold feeling of dread I get when I look at the battered old trainers I will put on to go downstairs and walk five minutes to the site of the protest, the pavement on which she was shot. I can't go and I can't stay home. My fear is so inevitable and matter-of-fact, so natural to my blood now, that I cannot even loathe myself for it.

I think, in the final moment of confrontation with my shoes, that I understand a bit of Sherine. Sherine who had been attacked with Farida on that night I ran into them on the street, Sherine who had already experienced those attacks by then, who would experience them again after.

Did she stare it in the face, every time? Did she make herself expect it—that she would be hurt, that it might be worse than last time? Or did she let herself hope that this time she would make it out safe? Which was more bearable? Which made it easier to get in her car, to drive to the square?

Omar pulls the door shut behind us, and I feel in my pocket for my ID one more time. We walk out into the sun and take the long way around the short block and a half to the protest site, where Shaimaa was killed. When I'm definitely out of time we part ways, and I bump into a girl I recognize from Opantish, Lina, and then Eman, also on their way to the protest.

"Do you have your IDs?" Eman asks, hugging us both.

We stand in the winter sunlight, a group of thirty women or so, silent, holding up signs. There are cameras everywhere. A group of policemen stand on the sidewalk opposite us.

We stand for almost an hour. There are some chants, some TV interviews. People are upset, but I don't feel rage, the rage that would have spread between us, would have rolled into a bigger crowd, would have moved us to march through the streets, into shouts of anger and demands for justice for Shaimaa, for how easily she was killed, for how easily any of us could be killed. The time for that is over. We stand fixed in place.

When I go home I don't feel angry. I feel tired and relieved that I am safe. I feel small.

20

July 1, 2013

11:00 a.m.

The morning after the confrontation in the metro station, T woke up from a sleep that was dreamless, which was what she'd hoped for. She washed her face and checked the TV room to see if anyone was asleep on the couch in there. There wasn't, but whoever had left last after the operation shut down had left the TV on mute. The ticker beneath the news anchor's face said "Egypt's second revolution."

She looked at last night's debris in the living room: piles of flyers and mugs and pens and phone chargers, the safety kits by the door, overflowing ashtrays, bags of leftover food that the intervention teams didn't get through.

She hadn't hesitated to offer her apartment when it became clear they needed to move out of Pierre's place. It had become too known, too open, too distracting in addition to now being a security risk.

"Are you sure you're ready for this?" Adam had asked her. "You shouldn't feel pressure to host the control room, and you can change your mind at any time. We'll find another space. But you, your sanity, I don't know, I'm less sure that we'd find it again …"

She smiled at him for never taking her crack-ups so seriously, for sharing her need for humor about the darkest black. But he knew—knew what she was like when she hadn't slept for days or when all she could do was sleep. Last winter, she had stayed with him for a few days when her anxiety had burst into a day of panic attacks. A terrible, repetitive loop of panic. Gasping for air, bent over, her voice lost. When it was over, her exhaustion and her anxiety medication made her slow, wordless.

He had cared for her like the gentlest nurse. When he sensed she was awake, he came into the bedroom with tea and buttered toast, or chicken soup with rice, only the homiest, simplest foods, the ones that remind you of being a sick child, remind you that there are people who would drop everything to make sure you get better. He spoke to her softly and made sure there was always a bottle of water by the bed.

On the day that she woke up and felt that getting out of bed might not send pain up from the ground all the way up to the crown of her head, she watched the light through the white curtains of the guest bedroom window. Then she got up and took a long bath, thinking about nothing. Afterward she fell asleep, wearing only a bathrobe he left hanging in the closet for her.

Now she sat down on her couch to do the rounds of checking email, Twitter, Facebook, and other messages. The news coverage and the discussion were polarized, describing what was happening as either a new wave of popular revolt or a military-backed coup. A false binary, she thought.

12:00 p.m.

I was rushing from the pharmacy to the Vodafone shop, going through the list of everything that needed refilling for the operation—markers, disinfectant, SIM cards—when I noticed someone waving a hand from just a couple of feet in front of me.

"Yasmin?" Azza said, eyes wide with concern.

"Oh, hi, Azza."

"Where are you going? Are you OK?"

Like so many Egyptians living abroad, Azza had left a life and a career in London to be part of the revolution in 2011.

"I'm fine, I'm sorry, I'm just distracted. I'm buying things for the operation—"

"For Opantish? I'll be there," she said. "I signed up after I saw the press release you guys put out."

We were standing on a street corner, sunlight dappled through a nearby tree as it hit the pavement around us. A group of teenagers who'd been leaning against a car nearby, eating sandwiches, burst into laughter.

"Will you be in the intervention teams?" Azza asks.

"No, in the operations room," I said.

"Oh, that big apartment with the view?"

"No, actually, we moved it because it was too dangerous there. I'm … I'm not supposed to say where it is."

"Wow, OK," Azza nodded. "Well, it's good to see you … I got a one-piece swimsuit to wear underneath my clothes, just like you told me."

We said good-bye, and I walked into the small, brightly lit Vodafone shop. The man in front of me in the line seemed to be in some sort of argument with the agent about his phone bill. It was thirty-four pounds, and he had counted it out in exact change. My own phone bill last month had been ten times as much.

The skin on his heels was thick, gray in the crevices that pressed down on the soles of his sandals. I stared at them as I listened to what he was saying.

"Curses on Morsi and on the Brotherhood that's bringing us all sinking down with them!" He took his receipt, and as he turned around to leave he looked at me as though I might have a response to match the strength of his feeling.

I kept my eyes on the agent in front of me and stepped up to the counter. "I need ten Sim cards and five basic Nokia phones," I said. The salesman raised his eyebrows. "I've got a group of friends arriving from abroad."

I reached into the roll of cash in my pocket to pay the bill. He smiled. "I hope they have a wonderful time. It's good to know tourists are still coming to Egypt."

10:00 p.m.

How had he gotten here?

Peter had always been quick to move, to get to the front line, to go where things were happening. Even if it wasn't immediately clear what the shape of the battle would be, he always knew he was there as a part of something larger than himself. Even when it was just twelve of them trapped in an alleyway, even when he got beat up by the cops on his own, it felt like the only place he could be. Even in the years before the uprising, when he was still in school and going to his first protests. Even when he was reporting on sectarian violence and the bombs that ripped apart churches in Upper Egypt, scavenging through grief and debris. He always knew what the fight was about, and who he was fighting with, and what against.

So how is he standing here with these people in the square, with his Opantish T-shirt on, and watching as a minibus pulls up through the crowd, and the people who get off are men wearing police band uniforms, and they are getting on the stage in front of the Mugamma and they are getting ready to perform to this crowd that is hysterical with nationalism?

He is standing near the Mohamed Mahmoud entrance to Tahrir. A group of about fifty people had come marching up to the entrance of the square, chanting for "Jeeka," holding a white banner with his face stenciled on it. "It was the police who killed Jeeka," they called out.

There is some pushing and yelling, from the people on the Tahrir side, the people standing with him, to keep the Jeeka group out.

Now there are glass bottles and rocks being thrown into the Jeeka group, and he sees three guys on the Tahrir side pulling out shotguns. Without thinking, he leaves Tahrir.

Interview: Peter, 2016

"I just started walking away from Tahrir and toward the people chanting for Jeeka. I don't remember making a decision. I didn't think about Opantish, about assault, about anything. It was like I was in a coma or a trance."

(Pause.)

"That was the last time I went to Tahrir."

1:30 a.m.

Leila looked at her team, some sitting on the pavement, others still standing, and counted twelve people. One guy had a bandage around his head from where a stick had cut him earlier that same day. She still had to go up to T's to debrief.

"I think we should call it a night," she said, and no one objected.

They headed back to the meeting point to hand off T-shirts and collect their stuff. Someone from the operations room handed her two bags—one filled with the watches, phones, car keys, and wallets that people had left before starting their shift, the other an empty duffel bag for the T-shirts to be collected in. Leila wanted to sit on the curb but she was afraid that, if she did, she wouldn't be able to get back up.

"Are we done?" Lina asked her. "That's it for today?"

She was standing next to her boyfriend Hamed, who was also on the team. Lina was about a head taller than him and beautiful in a deadpan, punk rock kind of way. She was on time to every meeting. Serious, quiet. Good on the ground, composed with survivors and with her teammates.

"Yes," Leila says. "You should go home."

Lina took her T-shirt off and turned it so that it was no longer inside out and then folded it neatly, as if it were freshly laundered, before putting it in the bag. "Thank you," she said to Leila with a small smile. "Good night," she said, turning away.

Leila looked through the bag to see how much stuff still needed to be collected. Three sets of keys, a wallet.

When she looked up, the couple was just a few feet away. Lina had collapsed into Hamed and she was crying. Her limbs looked like they could be made of paper, as though she couldn't hold them up on her own, and Hamed was holding her, and he might have been crying as well.

Not wanting to stare, Leila pretended to look back through the bag in her hands.

Interview: Leila, 2018

Leila: "All of the women were under enormous pressure not to show emotion while we worked. Lina had waited, she'd kept it together and double-checked that she was off duty before she let herself collapse. I felt so much respect for that."

Me: "Were you the only female captain?"

Leila: "Actually, I was never formally a captain. I had dreams, of course, of having all-women teams, several teams captained by women, and so on, and by the time the summer protests came around we had enough women to try and do this. We discussed it. But I felt that it wouldn't work with our dynamics on the street, that it would be seen as somehow … performative. Like, oh, look at these women making a show of leading mixed teams. So instead I—and other women—were never named captains as such, even though we were actually the ones in charge."

3:00 a.m.

Marwan didn't know how to calm himself down after operations anymore. He tried sitting at street cafés into the early hours of the morning. His heart raced, his knees moved up and down. He was so agitated he had to leave, mid-tea, mid-conversation.

"Wait, what, I thought you were giving me a ride," Ahmed called after him, but Marwan just waved him off, mumbling an apology.

He sat in his car, put his head on the steering wheel. A man came up and started to wipe the windshield clean.

He rolled down the window, "Leave it, leave it, I don't want it!" he said, and his own voice sounded alien to him. The old man looked at him flatly, without surprise, and walked away without a word.

He still had to drive to the toll booth, where he'd leave his car and then get a microbus to base, sneaking in before the dawn prayer.

He closed his eyes and counted backwards from one hundred. When he was down to seventy one of his legs stopped shaking. When he was down to twenty-eight both legs were still. He kept going all the way to zero.

Interview: Marwan, 2016

Me: "You use the word 'vulgar' a lot when you talk about Opantish. Why?"

Marwan: "My feeling was that it was a bunch of bodies attacking other bodies. They don't want anything. In clashes, we know that we've done something, and there is now a response from the state … but with Opantish I would leave the house feeling like I was just a body, and I'm going to a battle from the Middle Ages that I don't really understand.

"My sexual life was affected for a long time. I had a problem with my body and the body in front of me. What used to feel natural now made me nervous about myself. And I was never a guy who'd catcalled or anything like that, there was never anything I'd done to make me uneasy about myself. But I was very nervous, everything was loaded with a lot of things from outside of myself."

I have given myself license to imagine and write the innermost thoughts and feelings of people I worked with during some of the most heightened, extreme times of their lives. While it may be that there is no singular truth that can be claimed to this story, this history, as the pages grow it is clearer and clearer to me that I want everything in this book to *be true*.

Of all the individual stories that I could not fit into this book, perhaps the one I want to tell the most is the story of Marwan's double act, the overlap between his time in the military and his time with Opantish. I want to imagine the time he spent in solitary confinement during boot camp, when he talked back to an officer who was abusing a young conscript. He was locked up for ten days. "Military prison is more violent than regular prison," he says.

I want to imagine what it felt like to be dragged into sunlight, into open air, after ten days alone in a cramped cell. I want to describe the trainings he went through after his unit was transferred to a combat force ahead of June 30, simulating urban warfare, storming fake buildings, and the rising fear that he and the other conscripts would be ordered to open fire on protesters. I want to describe him sneaking away from military base to come to the square for Opantish, where he didn't wear his uniform, because if he were arrested with it on it could complicate his sentence.

But I cannot. It is too far from what I know and from the world of Opantish and Tahrir that I have shared with him. The details and the feelings that I can come up with are too wholly fiction. When I sit down with Marwan, we speak for three hours, but the details of his time in the military stay in the periphery, a reality that he references but does not describe.

21

July 2, 2013

Opantish was operating for the fourth day in a row.

The shifts in the control room were long, relentless. Tension filled the room slowly, like water dripping into a tank.

The calls kept coming in, headlines that kept accumulating, the beginnings of terrible stories that had no endings except the worst that we could imagine. All we could do was direct the teams on the ground and hope that they got there in time.

"My friend, she's gone, I can't see her anymore."

"Where are you? You mean you're not working in Ismailiyya? But they took her, it's happening, you mean you can't do anything?"

Farida gripped a phone in one hand as she made notes with the other. Then she kept it next to her, picking it up and looking at it every few seconds, as though to make sure it was still working.

"There are three women trapped in KFC, two of us are inside with them."

"My teammate's head is bleeding, can someone take us to the hospital?"

"We need more flares."

Eman was leaning against the bookshelf in the living room, taking a call. Farida and T sat on the couch in front of her.

"That group that was stuck in KFC got out, and one of the women wants to go to the hospital," Eman said after hanging up.

"There was a knife?" Farida asked.

"There wasn't any knife, or if there was we didn't hear about it."

Drip.

"OK, so how many of them were there? Three?"

"There were two women," Eman said.

"And they were stripped?"

"I'm not sure."

"How many men were there?"

"I don't know, really, we might get this information from the team at the end of the night, but I don't have it now." Eman's voice was cool.

Drip.

"Who's taking her to the hospital? Nahya?"

"The car from Garden City, actually. I think they went down the corniche and got there pretty fast," Habiba said.

"OK, so that's car three," T said, looking at the chart across from her. "I'll follow up with them."

Suzy noted all of this down in her laptop.

"So, wait, are you sure there wasn't a knife?" Farida asked again.

There was a pause.

"I'm gonna call Doctors Without Borders. Maybe they can send someone to meet them at the hospital," Habiba said.

My body leaned away from Farida, my weight pressed against the end of the couch, my arm reached over the end of it, as if to get away.

Drip.

"Where did I hear that there was a knife?" Farida said again, to no one.

My voice, angry and sharp: "There is no knife, let's stop talking about a knife. Nobody said there was a knife."

"Are we not allowed to ask questions now?" she pushed back. "What's wrong with you? Why do you have such an attitude?"

I looked straight ahead and didn't reply.

I didn't notice that Suzy, sitting at a table to the side of the room with her laptop, looked distraught.

"OK, I think we need to talk about the rest of the night and who to send home," T said. "Some of these guys have been down there for six hours."

Later that night, standing in the kitchen with Eman and looking for some kind of absolution, I apologized for losing my cool.

She took a sandwich out of a bag of food that the intervention teams hadn't gotten through. She shrugged as she peeled back the plastic wrap. "Look, I don't give a shit about people keeping cool heads or not. What matters is that the work gets done."

She paused.

"This sandwich is disgusting," she said, taking a few more bites before wrapping it back up. "Come on, let's see what we're gonna do about tomorrow."

2:00 a.m.

Everyone who was still around gathered in the living room. Suzy moved over from the table she'd been at all night and sat on the floor with the laptop.

"OK, we intervened in eighty-seven cases today," she started.

"Damn," Habiba said.

"How many calls did we get?" I asked.

"One hundred and twenty-seven," she said, and I noticed that she was avoiding making eye contact with me.

Farida had left.

The military has given the Brotherhood an ultimatum: either step down from the presidency or be removed by force.

While reading an early draft of this book on the subway in 2018, this is the point at which Farida had to stop. When she got out at her station she had a panic attack on the platform. Her books and papers spilled out of her bag and onto the floor as she crouched down. The train sped away. The legs of strangers rushed past her, although a few people stopped and leaned down to ask if she was OK.

July 3, 2013

When I woke up the next morning, my body felt like lead. I opened the shutters to let the light in and quickly closed the windows again to keep in the air conditioning. I went back to bed, picked up my phone, ignored the text messages from my mother, and went straight into my email. There were new emails on the Opantish core group, mostly about logistics. There was one from Suzy, titled "Operations Room."

"I have talked with a few of the others."

"We want this to be a safe space."

"Some people are taking a managerial tone ..."

I put the phone down and burrowed my face into a pillow.

Everything around me was big and swirling. The coup that was in motion, the square that was celebrating it, the unknown future, the certainty of more attacks. But all I could feel in that moment was guilt for my misplaced aggression toward Farida, of all people.

I wasn't even annoyed at the reprimand of Suzy's email, because
she was right.

There was a version of myself that had been calm through the
chaos of January 25, but I didn't know how to find her anymore,
and I didn't know who else I could be in that place, in the nerve
center of information about injured volunteers, hospitals refus-
ing to admit women, about a microbus without license plates that
snatched three women near Tahrir, all of it a background to the
number of attacks, a total which could only ever rise. Being away
from the square didn't give us a feeling of safety or, if it did, it
was in equal measure to an anxiety similar to what comes from
consuming news of a nearby disaster—except in this case we were
also supposed to be directly helping, and we weren't ever really
sure we were.

I went downstairs to make a cup of coffee. Nahya was still
asleep on the daybed.

"Come out in the intervention with me," she'd said to me the
day before. "It's really different now. There are so many of us. It
doesn't feel scary the way that it used to."

As I waited for the water to boil up through the steel percolator,
I decided. Standing in the kitchen, I typed an email to the group:

*I will wash the T-shirts and bring them to T's, and I will meet H
about the lights in Mohamed Mahmoud. But after that, I think I need
a break from the Operations Room—it is in the most capable hands of
Habiba. I will be on intervention tonight.*

When the coffee was ready, I hit Send.

Later that morning, I emptied out a black weekend bag that
had been sitting by the door of the apartment for weeks. Beneath
the clothes and flip-flops and unread books there were bits of sand
carried back from a trip to the north coast, evidence of a different
kind of summer.

I counted the T-shirts as I piled them into the bag. Eighty-two. They had taken three loads in the small machine, and dried within a couple of hours in the July sun. I threw two of them out, one that had been cropped short and another with a blood stain on the sleeve—the wearer probably didn't even notice when they threw the shirt into the pile at the end of the night. I zipped up the bag, pushing the top down with my knee to be able to close it all the way.

I had bought a pair of loose trousers specifically for the square made of a cheap, sturdy material that I didn't care about ruining. I couldn't bear the thought of wearing leggings underneath them in the heat.

Farida's voice came into my head, with a warning from months ago: *Wear a belt, Yasmin, this isn't a joke.*

8:00 p.m.

There were about twenty people in my team, stationed in the alley next to Hardee's. They stood in small groups or sat on the curb. Puddles of street water sent up a stagnant smell from the ground around us.

We were waiting for a phone call from the operations room or a message from one of the four scouts stationed in balconies with different vantage points of the square, telling us an attack had been spotted in our quadrant.

The cheap fabric of my trousers was thick and itchy in the heat. My stomach felt full of cigarette smoke and adrenaline. I tried to draw calmness from the conversation around me. Someone was talking about looking for an apartment to rent. Someone else was planning a trip to Mexico. We could have been anywhere. The exploding fireworks in the sky, which started while the sun was still up, could have been for a holiday or a wedding rather than a military coup.

I kept looking to the team captain, Tarek, who had large green eyes and an impossibly young-looking face, waiting to see him answer his phone or hear him say, "It's time to go."

A girl sitting on the floor near me, the sleeves of her T-shirt pulled up to her shoulders for coolness in this off-duty moment, introduced herself as Aya and told me she had gone to school with my younger brother. That made her barely two years out of college. My brother had volunteered in a field clinic in Tahrir during the eighteen days of the revolution's first wave but kept his distance after that, feeling failed and alienated. Everything that came after the victory of ousting Mubarak looked, to him, like chaos. He saw no majesty in the crowds of perseverant protesters, hurling rocks at the police who had shot them in the eyes, in the stubborn insistence on justice for the dead, in the belief that dignity could not be found in compromising with brutal forces. I'd told him what I told myself—no, what I believed—what Nahya and T and everyone else said, and what I'd felt pass like a current between all of us, that revolution is not only about taking power but that it is between people, within them.

Aya and I were still talking, and suddenly it was time to move; everyone was getting up and forming into two lines. Nahya was in line in front of me, and we started to push through the sea of people. Once we were in the square, it was impossible for anyone to speak over the noise. I didn't know where we were going, didn't know anything about what I would find. All I knew was what I was supposed to do. Nahya turned and looked at me, nodded, and then reached back and took my hand in hers, and I was surprised by how small it felt. But I also knew that she was pulling me outside of myself and into that moment, that place, the choice that we had all had to make.

☙

While working on this book, I realized that I did not remember the rest of the sequence of events from my experience with the intervention teams. I did not write down what happened beyond this point, so there is no document to trigger my memory.

My memory gathers and slips away more or less as I expect it to throughout my experiences in the operations room, at meetings, even walking in the streets during this period—and then is abruptly silent and inaccessible at the moment that I enter the square to intervene. Most of the work I did for Opantish was logistical: buying material, making lists, delegating tasks, scheduling, making phone calls. This is the work of analysis and rationalizing, of making sense of what should be done and when, of menial tasks, almost all of which were executed several stories above the square. The control room is an act of management done within a physical realm and using a set of tools that are familiar: phones, paper, pen, the internet, time for a conversation with others. It is of a completely different and almost oppositional nature to the unpredictable danger, the somatic mess, and the existential stakes of the work happening below. The two happen in a relationship of need and tension with one another: need, because they needed one another to exist, and tension because each site positioned our thinking, feeling bodies into distinct ways of dealing with crisis that became antagonistic to one another.

Leila told me in an interview years later, "At some point, there was an inability for us as people on intervention to really deal with people in the operations room. I hated going up there, I really hated it."

I know that I was not attacked that night, because the events and conversations after that day, and working on this text, would have been different. I've often talked about being spared the violence—someone would have told me, or let it slip on their face, if I were wrong.

It's possible that my memory was not always blocked. It's a memory of the core experience of Opantish—this act of people, of women, saving one another—and it is this act and what it means in the context of everything happening around it that I've spent so long trying to understand. In the years of research and thinking and writing, I have run so many circles around it that I may have made my own direct memory of it inaccessible.

Perhaps my experience was the same as it was for so many others —the extreme physicality of a crowd, fear, safety in numbers, the profound and fleeting experience of connecting with a survivor. Perhaps it was different and less happened. Or more.

22

July 4, 2013

I hadn't expected the lights—fierce, flooding onto me from just a few feet away, even though the mid-morning sun was blazing above the hotel balcony near Tahrir, where we were filming. The questions would come through the earpiece in my right ear, which felt dangerously close to falling out. I wasn't supposed to look at any of the faces around me: not the cameraman, smiling and patient, or the friendly producer, stepping into the hotel room to take phone calls every couple of minutes.

President Morsi had been arrested by the army the day before, and no one knew where they were keeping him. After those celebrations, we thought the square would be calmer, and so it was the first day in nearly a week that we weren't operating. We all needed a break.

I had put my clothes—the itchy trousers, the swimsuit, the hoodie—in the washing machine and taken a long shower. I put on a blue top and a long white skirt. I thought about the skirt for a while.

It was the beginning of the day, and the catcalls from peddlers on the sidewalk and men walking and cycling past as I walked to the studio were more explicit than usual. As if there was something left over from the night before, injecting confidence and aggression into their gazes.

"Thirty seconds, love," the producer said.

I tried not to look at the lights, tried to keep my eyes on the cool darkness of the camera lens.

And then we were on, and I could hear the presenter—a woman, heavy accent—in the London studio.

"… horrific attacks against female protesters … plagued this dramatic political week in Cairo … from the heart of it, in Tahrir, we have Yasmin … part of a brave group …"

"Yasmin, who do you and your group think are behind these attacks? Are these men hired by the Muslim Brotherhood to disrupt the protests against the Morsi administration?"

The slick answer: the Egyptian government and security apparatus has used sexual violence against protesters for years. On top of this, we have a deep societal problem when it comes to harassment—there is almost total impunity for sexual harassment and assault on the streets. Even if someone has hired a bunch of thugs to start attacking women, you wouldn't have the kind of mobs—of hundreds of men at a time—forming so quickly if there wasn't this problem. People are joining in. And the state knows this very well.

After I took the earpiece out and left the studio, unsure what to do with my strangely empty day, I thought, *We will never know the truth.*

The days and weeks that immediately followed the coup felt like a strange sort of waiting time. But what were we waiting for? For the showdown between the Brotherhood and the army to be over? For us to have a role again?

Nahya stayed with me often. I gave her my bedroom and slept on the daybed in the living room.

"Why are you so weird about this? Let's just share the bed," she said.

"I wake up a lot, and I want to turn on the lights and read without waking you. It's better for me, it's more comfortable," I said.

It was true that I was waking up a lot in the night, but I wasn't reading. I hadn't been able to read for weeks. Instead I stared at the ceiling, or at the window, or at the bookshelves. I tried not to check Twitter and Facebook.

The level of debate in the press and among secular groups had plummeted into an "us" and "them," us being the imaginary of regular society, and them being hardcore Morsi and Brotherhood supporters. The "us" was rallying behind the armed forces— the oldest, most stable political actor. "They" were portrayed as intransigent, unwilling to accept that the people had spoken against them, harping on about having won the presidency legitimately.

The city's air was heavy, threatening. People on the street were jumpy, nervous. Brotherhood supporters and others opposed to the president's ouster had set up camps in Nahda Square and in front of the Raba'a al-'Adawiyya mosque in Nasr City. Fear was being pumped out of TV and radio news stations, spelled out in headlines: "The Brotherhood are ready to seek revenge for their president"; "Egypt faces civil war." I knew it wasn't true, these were manipulations, but I could still see that the city was different, I could still feel the threat I wanted to dismiss. Every moment felt unusual, dislodged from regular time and consequence.

Near my apartment, a boy of about twelve was walking on the sidewalk toward Nahya and me, carrying a stick about five feet long. As we came closer to one another he lifted it up, moved as if to strike us. We were far enough away that I didn't flinch as I sometimes had in the past when men swerved their cars as though to hit me on the pavement or when they suddenly shouted loud animal noises at me, the sheer volume jolting me into a reaction. For the boy carrying the stick, for all those men in cars and on bikes or on their feet, scaring me had been a joke. I had been a joke.

In that quarter second in which I usually would have flinched, I watched Nahya as she sized up this man-boy, scanning him for harm, for unpredictability. She squared herself toward him and shouted, "Are you gonna hit us? Go ahead! Go ahead and hit us!"

He looked at her blankly and half-heartedly raised the stick once more, an imitation of himself.

"Go ahead, you think that makes you tough?"

As he walked away, he muttered something under his breath.

We continued walking, Nahya wearing a satisfied look on her face.

23

T and Eman were standing outside the meeting room smoking when I arrived.

"This is fucking bullshit," T said. Her cheeks were flushed with anger. Eman shook her head.

The organizers' meeting being held in the room behind them was to decide whether Opantish would operate during a rally the military was calling for a few days later. They had asked people to go out into the streets and give them a mandate to "deal with terrorism," meaning the Muslim Brotherhood and its supporters.

"What happened?" I asked.

"Had we not decided that it would be up to a vote by *all* the volunteers, whether we go down for Sisi's rally?" T asked.

"We did."

"Yes, we did, and we sent like a zillion emails, and we talked about it for hours. And we set up the vote, and we asked them all to do it, and the majority said yes, let's go out."

"OK ... "

"Well, now, these pashas in the room behind me have decided

to override all of this, override everyone, and have no operation on Thursday."

"The worst part," Eman said, "is that we're going back on our word to the volunteers. We told them it would be up to them, and now we're just doing what we want anyway."

"Did you guys say all this, in there?"

"Yes," T says. "And I cursed, and I told them that we're being fascists. If we're gonna be fascists, then let's just be fascists, why are we pretending that we're letting people in on decisions, why pretend that we don't want to be top-down? Let's just say it: we're running the show, and whoever doesn't like the way we decide things can leave."

In the room, there were about ten people around the table.

"So how are we going to tell the volunteers?" Habiba asked.

"If we're canceling we have to tell them right away," Eman said, her voice firm and her words quick. "We're going to get a lot of shit for this, a lot of shit. A lot of the volunteers are really keen to go out. We need to at least be up front as soon as possible."

"They can still go out, Eman," Seif said. "They can form their own groups and go. People have done it before. We just can't have an operation. We've got clear messages from the police: they're going to be on the lookout for 'harassment patrols.' We can't be there in any real way."

She didn't reply.

"Also I don't think we *should*," Habiba said. "This is a military rally. We've maintained this whole time that we are of this revolution, that we're feminist. We can't do this, not on that day."

"I'm with you, believe me I am, I understand. But they just don't all feel that way, and this is no longer just about us, there are dozens, hundreds of people who are just as invested in this as we are, they've put just as much on the line, and it's fucked up that we're ignoring what they want," Eman said. "We're going to lose them."

Adam had been quiet so far. "Do we know their rationale? The people who want to go?"

"Let me pull up an email," Eman said. "This is from Attiya, who's been with us since January, and he's one of the most committed. He says: 'Regardless of our own political leanings, I don't think the women who will be out in the square on Thursday deserve our help any less than the women that have been out for the revolution.'"

"I'm sorry, but that isn't the whole picture," Habiba said. "Thursday's rally is called for by the state. Come on, this is the minister of defense asking for a *popular mandate* to combat *terrorism*! It's basically a blood pact. The police will be there to protect it, the army will be there. This is not the same as the protests we started from. This is their rally, let them be responsible for it."

The argument went around the same circle a couple of times before the meeting ended, maintaining the decision not to work on Thursday. As T got up to leave, Seif said, "We have to move the toys," meaning the weapons. "They can't stay in your house, and whatever's in the cars has to be moved too. The risk of getting caught is too high, downtown is swarming with security."

The group of organizers at that meeting was more or less the same group that had been running Opantish since January; many of them had been in the core team since the group was formed in November. After it was all over, every female organizer I interviewed talked about how a small group of people—the more radical, the louder activists—monopolized the larger group's identity.

Some of the people who hold those voices themselves said as much: that in their militancy they drowned out other perspectives.

Interviews, 2017, 2016, 2015

Rana was one of the very first organizers of Opantish. She was the one who called a meeting of activists and rights workers after her own assault in November 2012, to organize a civilian force focusing on harassment and assault. It was also she who, in the charged debriefing after the anniversary attacks, raised the question of women's presence on the ground. After that, she stepped aside from the organizing team and joined the main body of volunteers.

Rana: "I stepped aside from the core group because I didn't think I would be of good use anymore. But, at the same time, I was very frustrated. Like so many revolutionary groups, we had become snobbish and exclusive, only trusting friends or friends of friends. And we didn't want to get involved in any real political work. You say you're radical, but you blame everyone else for not being radical enough. It becomes an ideological fight, while people are getting hurt and killed.

"It was astonishing that they didn't want to involve the judicial system at all, but at the same time we were always responding to statements by the government and issuing press releases addressing them. So why not do full legal advocacy? Every time I suggested this, I was told it was a 'reformist' idea … There was too much intellectualizing … I always thought of myself as both a revolutionary and a human rights defender. This wasn't about whether I believed in the government. It was about women getting assaulted and I thought we should use all means available to fight that."

Eman and some of the other organizers had a longer-term view of what Opantish could do about sexual violence, beyond Tahrir and even beyond the revolution. In one of my earliest interviews for this book, Eman told me that we lost and alienated people by insisting on radical positions that they did not all necessarily share.

"You have hundreds of volunteers, and I mean really committed people, who are ready to mobilize on this issue ... when we set ourselves up to be unable to work outside the revolution, we just lost all that," she said.

Three years after that July meeting, T talked to me about the essay "The Tyranny of Structurelessness," about power relations within radical feminist groups in the United States in the 1960s, written by a long-term activist. The essay describes how movements that organized themselves explicitly without leaders, without hierarchal structures, often end up being run by an unacknowledged, or at least unaccountable, group that hoards all decision-making power. The essay argues that in order to be democratic, movements need some formal structure.

A Google search brings up anarchist critiques of the essay, calling it a red herring, drawing attention away from the formal organizations where real tyranny is practiced, and that the problem the essay describes is due not to collective decision-making but to people who are unsure of themselves, people who cannot navigate a world of social relationships freed from written rules, roles, and formalities.

Opantish did have an organizational structure and a division of labor, and it was known that a core group of organizers, actually called the Core, made strategic decisions often without consulting other volunteers. We did, at some point, discuss democratizing in a few different ways: rotating people out of the Core and bringing new people in, systematizing ways of communicating with and consulting volunteers beyond general meetings. But we never managed to do this.

Opantish burned bright when it was active: the whole organism would come to life quickly, getting people on the ground and speaking to the media. In the times in between, the times during which a group might make structural changes, people were often too busy with other work, or burned out, or unable to engage for whatever reason. There were a few changes in the core group over the year or so that Opantish was active: some people quit the group or moved abroad, and some new people did come in. But many of those who set the agenda and the tone of the group remained until the end. We were unable to let go of our control.

For T, Nahya, Habiba, and so many others, Opantish was about saving women but it was also about a strategic political ambition. It was about using a militant feminist approach to finally bring the issue of gender liberation to the center of the revolution. There was a fear that a change in leadership would turn the movement into one that was more violent or less political or more segregated. That it would take on, for example, a strategy of segregating protest spaces, or appeal to paternalist tropes about protecting women, or embrace a narrative of female victimhood—that Opantish would, in short, stop focusing on the activity of women themselves.

Alongside her self-critique, T said, "In the end, all we had in common with many of the volunteers, with our supporters, was a belief that women shouldn't be raped in the streets. And that's not a very high bar."

What did it mean if a large portion of the hundreds of volunteers didn't share the same politics and saw what was happening as simply a humanitarian intervention? Where is the line between protecting a principle and monopolizing a movement, limiting it? Is there a line?

Opantish faced the same bind that so many revolutionary initiatives find themselves in at one point or another, especially as the political possibilities for the revolution began constricting: what we believed we were about also meant that we were at the end of what we could actively do. Some called this integrity, others called it puritanism. By the time the coup had unfolded, it was too late. Everything changed, irrevocably, with a ground-shifting violence that society has still not confronted, even as I write this many years later.

24

The city went to bed, and when we woke up we had become a place where one of the worst massacres in modern history had taken place.

I found out about the massacre at Rab'a al-'adawiyya from Twitter. For weeks, the authorities had been talking about wiping out the camps of Brotherhood supporters. That was the language used in the media: not *disperse* or *dismantle* but *wipe out*, *eradicate*. *Empty*.

At dawn, security forces moved in on the sit-in with APCs and guns. By the time the city was awake, by the time I looked at my phone, the blood was in pools, bodies were burning, and the death toll being reported was in the hundreds.

The television flashed with images of the dead, of the tanks, of people panicking. Commentators rushed to support security forces. *Brotherhood* and *terrorism* were used interchangeably.

At least 825 people were killed that morning. Men, women, children, reporters. Brotherhood leaders and supporters, people who didn't support the Brotherhood but were against Morsi's removal by coup, people who had said they were willing to die and others who did not.

I have to spell it out plainly like that, because what happened afterward was every attempt to obfuscate the basic wrongness of it, to turn mass murder into an act of patriotism or *necessity*, and it is terrifying how small the distance between the two turned out to be.

Journalists were killed, including a Sky News cameraman named Mike Dean who was probably in the hotel room where I had filmed the interview about Opantish. I don't think it was him filming me, but it could have been. I don't think it was him fixing my earpiece before we started, but it could have been.

The terror of the massacre itself was used to forbid criticism of the state and its tactics. A few people tried to keep writing, to keep cutting through the state's narrative. The words *chauvinistic, xenophobic,* and *fascist* were heard for a little while among the secular left and what remained of the Brotherhood, whose leadership was quickly being hunted down and jailed.

One night late that summer, I was at a long dinner table covered in half-empty dishes and bottles. A gathering of friends to pass the long curfewed evenings. The talk turned to Raba'a, and to the deaths.

"The Brotherhood needed to be stopped," someone at the end of the table said.

Words were turning what should be incomprehensible into something calculable, rational. Words plucked from the discourse rushing around the airwaves.

"They had weapons there, at the camp in Raba'a. They were getting ready to start a war," the same voice was now saying. It was Azza.

I couldn't believe it. Azza of the one-piece-swimsuit, Azza who signed up right away, Azza who dropped out of a whole life and career in London to come and be part of the revolution. I didn't speak, because I was afraid of what I would say.

Around this time, I noticed that I'd stopped finishing my sentences. I started speaking in half-expressed thoughts that would trail off into silence or the twisting pitch of a question mark. It wasn't that I had given up on words; I felt that I needed them more now, maybe needed them too much. But I was also afraid of them, afraid of using the wrong ones, as though an idea that was poorly expressed could never be corrected and would cause irreparable harm. Everything had become sticky and heavy with meaning, and right and wrong and horror and understanding had gotten lost in the sticky heaviness. When I tried to pick them out, to find a thread to grab on to, I fell flat and stuck under the weight. The words were lost, the ones that came were not precise, not correct. So I gave up, leaving sentences open, hoping that the person I was speaking to would understand, somehow, what it was I was trying to say. If they did not, then it would be the fault of silence, not of my mischosen words, and maybe that would be less harmful.

I could not keep myself from beginning these stillborn sentences, though. I preferred, in the end, to be caught in a moment of reaching, of trying, of rounding my mouth around the words that I could find. I felt that giving up on the attempt would be a kind of death.

25

November 2013

Opantish went out once more after the massacre. It was the anniversary of the 2011 street battle of Mohamed Mahmoud, a four-day confrontation with police at one of the main entrances to Tahrir. Each team voted on whether to go out. Going back and looking at the email threads, half the responses seemed to be for it, and the other half were people saying they didn't think we should go but that they would be there if the group decided to intervene. There were fears of random arrests, and word had reached us that the police were after organized "vigilante groups."

"We definitely shouldn't wear our T-shirts," someone wrote.

By that point, we'd printed new T-shirts that said, "A Street Safe for All" rather than "A Midan Safe for All."

According to the emails, Eman and I were in charge of emergency logistics—getting people to safe houses and the like. We set up the operations room in the offices of Mosireen, the media collective where many of the organizers also worked.

There were no mob assaults that night. News reports tell me that thousands of protesters, opposed to both the Brotherhood and the military, filled Tahrir. In the evening, clashes broke out; one person was killed, and fifty were injured.

During this period, I'd taken to wearing an oversized gray hoodie whenever I went out. I went on a small march a day before the Opantish operation, to mark the anniversary of Jeeka's death—Jeeka, the handsome boy killed by the cops.

A crowd of about one hundred people gathered in the small alley of his family's home in Abdeen. Despite the months of silence since the coup and the massacre, the chants came easily —"Down, down with military rule!" Jeeka's family and their neighbors filled the street and the balconies above, which were draped in white banners with his stenciled, chanting face. What had he been saying?

We marched to Abdeen Square. Once on the main road, away from the world of Jeeka's family, the balconies were full of a different kind of spectator. They threw plant pots down on us. Some liquid splashed down in front me.

"Bleach," a guy walking next to me said. "Don't look up."

Any public gathering that wasn't explicitly in support of the military had become suspicious, intolerable. "Enough already, you've ruined the country!" people yelled from their windows, from their cars.

In Abdeen Square, there was a small stage with its back to the royal palace. Families of the murdered spoke from here—the old men who had lost their children, the mothers in black, the siblings—and the crowd tried to be respectful and contain its restlessness.

Arwa was standing next to me as we listened to a young woman whose brother was killed. "We owe it to the dead to keep the revolution going," the woman said. She wore a veil and spoke to the crowd directly. Her voice was clear, but she didn't shout or chant, and I remember thinking that her anger was more moving because it was controlled.

I realized Arwa was crying. Not a few tears but a whole wet, shining face full of them. "I can't believe that this is all that we can do for them," she said.

I walked back toward my house, hoping no one would recognize me from the march. I passed a café where I used to spend time while I was at university a few blocks from here, newly charmed with the old haunts of downtown, the histories they did not flaunt, the stories you had to know from an old person or an old book.

I'd also felt harassed and oppressed by these streets as I tried to move my body through them. Later, the revolution made me feel freed by them, scared of them, protective of them, full of anger toward them, nostalgic for earlier moments spent in them. The buildings and the gravel pulsed with all of these conflicting feelings—these realities—that they had held. But right now they looked flat and cold. Lifeless.

Part IV

It's like we all went out and we did this huge, crazy thing together, and then we went home and we never talked about it again.

—Habiba, 2015

It is perfectly possible—indeed, it is far from uncommon—to go to bed one night, or wake up one morning, or simply walk through a door one has known all one's life, and discover, between inhaling and exhaling, that the self one has sewn together with such effort is all dirty rags, is unusable, is gone: and out of what raw material will one build a self again?

—James Baldwin, *Nothing Personal*, 1964

26

There is nowhere to run but on this machine. I watch the red digits on the panel. I feel an extra satisfaction, visualize a drop of dopamine seeping through my brain, when my eye catches the mileage as it goes up: 3.3 to 3.4, 4.7 to 4.8 … I will make it to 8 miles today.

A bad action movie is playing on the television screen above me. In my ears is the same playlist I've been running to for weeks. I can't be bothered to change it. Katy Perry switches to Beyoncé, Lady Gaga gives way to Michael Jackson. When I run I only want big pop music, the kind that we dance to in spite of ourselves.

Halfway through the sixth mile, a woman wearing a baseball cap over her straightened, black hair gets on the machine to my left. She walks for a bit, then breaks into a light jog, then more walking. She is talking into her headset the whole time. I can't hear what she's talking about, but I feel her sidelong glances every few minutes.

Mile seven now. I've never run this far on a machine.

Baseball cap is now leaving. She gives me a smile. I half-wave as I wipe the sweat off my face with the bottom of my T-shirt. I want to go faster, but I know I should save that till the very end, the final stretch. My feet are flying off the moving rubber up the light incline to nowhere, and I still want to go faster. It doesn't matter if I'm running in place, it's not about direction. I want to create my own version of speed, my own pounding rhythm of heartbeat and breath and step. I want to move through a different version of time—maybe the seconds move faster, or maybe there are less hours in the day. Maybe then I would be released from the feeling that we are all sinking, so slowly that we don't even notice. The ground is rising, and soon we will be underneath it, and it will be too late to reach for each other or for anyone still above ground. No one will even see us go.

Seven and a half miles. I push the speed button up. My playlist has ended and I don't want to start it again—I'm afraid that the movement might disrupt my coordination and make me trip. I am tired. I think of the food I've eaten, try to summon the energy from it into my legs. I hear the whirring, now, of the motor, the impact of my feet, my breath. The trainer on duty walks past, glances at me with a neutral expression.

Don't talk to me. Please. Don't.

He keeps walking.

I make sure I watch the red 7.9 turn to eight and as soon as it does, I slow down. I run slowly for a few minutes, then walk, wiping the sweat off my face, my arms.

I've been bumping into things a lot: doors, tables, walls. I don't know where I end, what my outlines are. My body seems to have become separate from me, and its sense of its own dimensions has become distorted. It seems to no longer think that its movements have any consequence in the world, as though it were no longer a solid thing that could collide, disrupt. I feel that this melting of my borders has caused me to lose whatever grace I once had.

On my way up the stairs to the changing rooms, I run into the trainer. "You know, you should let us get you on some weights," he says. "If you run so much without building the muscles up, you'll end up very weak."

"It's OK, thanks, maybe next time," I say quickly and keep walking up the stairs.

Maybe one day there will be a reason to be strong again. For now, all I want is to escape, to be in this accelerated version of time, even just for an hour every day. If all it did to my body was burn it down to scraggly muscles, to fibrous, unsculpted tissue hanging off of the bones, it wouldn't matter, because we have already lost.

27

About a year after the coup, I left Cairo for New York without much of a plan, just a searching.

My body felt different after I left. Softer, rounder. My clothes all seemed wrong, like someone had suddenly switched a light on and I was seeing them for the first time.

On the Fourth of July, I was invited to an indoor "barbeque" at a friend of a friend's house. I was glad for the invitation, for something to do on the public holiday. I wore a red linen dress that I had stopped wearing in Cairo.

I bought a bottle of wine, spending what I would later learn was more time and money on it than I needed to for this kind of invitation.

There were about six people there when I arrived, including a gregarious hostess with shiny dark hair all the way down her back, who greeted me warmly and put the wine down next to the other bottles.

"When did you get to New York?" my friend Raphael asked after hugging me hello.

"Just a few days ago."

He introduced me to his friends—"She just moved here from Cairo!"

One of them, a handsome, preppy-looking guy named Dan, asked, "So what's happening there, with the Muslim Brotherhood and everything?"

I wasn't sure what this meant. Did he mean the crackdown against the Brotherhood? Or did he think that the Brotherhood were still in power?

"Well, Sisi just got elected, but he and the army have been running the country since last year," I said, worrying that I was sounding patronizing. "The Brotherhood are in deep shit, they're killing them and locking them up."

"Is it just them that they're going after?"

"No, they're arresting anyone who speaks out. Including, you know, my friends."

I don't know if there's a particular reason I said that last part, bringing the tragedy to sit heavy and awkward in the room. Maybe it was simply because it was true. In the discomfort that followed, Dan turned his eyes away from me and to the television screen and kept them there.

In the last hour of daylight, we set out to the riverfront to wait for the fireworks. It was packed with rows of people, and policemen moved within and around the crowds. The group settled on a spot to stand. Nearby was a young couple, college-age, maybe even younger. Both were clean-cut, Latinx, and almost painfully good-looking.

He was standing behind her, and he kept smoothing down her hair, which was very long and perfectly straight, and kissing the top of her head, putting his hands around her waist. She was looking at her phone a lot and then turning her head up to say things to him. He was clearly in a particular kind of love with her, a blinding, consuming kind of feeling that people can only live in when they're either very young or trying to change or save themselves.

I couldn't stop looking at them out of the corner of my eye. It had been so long since I'd seen something that could exist between people on their own terms and as its own force, not shaped by the euphoria of collective power or the silencing, crushing effect of defeat, the constant swings of the revolution that had pushed and pulled people toward each other and then apart, and into and out of themselves too.

The fireworks started, and I wondered whether we could spot the places on the bridge where they were being shot out into the sky. With each exploding sound, I hid the flinches in my shoulders, forced my feet to stay in place, tried to imagine roots growing out from my legs through the soles of my feet and into the ground. I realized I couldn't run from here even if I wanted to, even if I decided I didn't care about embarrassing myself in front of Raphael and his friends. The crowd was too tightly packed.

Don't be a caricature of traumas you didn't even know you had. Don't be weak. Stand still, and then go home.

A few weeks later, I stood on the beach at an engagement party next to a friend I've known for many years. Above us fireworks burst out, again, one after the other, and I couldn't guess where they were coming from.

This time I couldn't hide my flinches the way I'd done before, in Brooklyn. I gripped the sand with my toes but within a few moments my shoulders had rolled forward and my neck had bent down and it wasn't a dramatic crouch but it was a crouch, a completely involuntary and irresistible reaction to the sounds falling around us. Something was happening that I could not stop. I had once been in control of these muscles, had moved my limbs right into crowds or front lines. Now this body didn't care what I thought of the scenes around me or what I wanted it to do. My limbs had colluded with some part of my brain that I could not control and had decided that they'd had enough.

I said to the friend standing next to me, "I'm having trouble with the noise, I think I'll go inside," and his eyes filled with sympathy. I still can't be around fireworks, and it seems a trivial loss, as weightless as the dancing colors themselves.

28

March 2015

I took a job with an NGO in Manhattan, researching press freedom in Egypt and the region, the different ways that reporting puts journalists at risk of jail or kidnapping or murder. It allows me to feel like I'm still contributing to a larger search for justice, to stay connected to the details of the atmosphere in Cairo.

I speak to journalists or their relatives, try to verify the details of their stories.

"What are the charges against you?"

"Were you reporting at the protest or were you taking part in it?"

"Do you know where your husband's body is?"

"Has your brother been kidnapped by militants before?"

"I am sorry, we can't help with resettlement."

My phone lights up in the night with messages from Egypt, Sudan, Libya, sometimes Syria by way of Turkey. People in the form of thumbnail photos reaching out to me in a still-sleeping New York, sometimes thinking this organization, whose stature is connected to America's power, would be able to help. Sometimes it is. I learn to switch my phone off when I go to bed, then I learn not to look at it until I am in the office, then I learn to ask for a separate phone for work.

While the most violent cases—the murders and the kidnapping—are from other countries, it's in Egypt that a near-total blackout on independent reporting hit. The number of journalists in jail doubles, then quadruples. Egypt starts to appear like a monstrous spectacle of repression—repression beyond reason, an open-ended counterrevolution.

People ask me, sometimes with enthusiasm, about what I'm doing, what I'm working on, why I moved to the city, where from. Sometimes they want to ask questions about the revolution and why it had *failed*, about what *the situation* is like *over there* right now. Sometimes the person I am speaking with will suddenly start sounding like a news anchor, adopting a slight frown on their face as they speak, as if this would make them seem more serious, more sincere.

I don't know how to approach this recent, ongoing history with the old words. I feel like I'm trying to explain a color—not a relational color, not burgundy or turquoise. It's like trying to explain white.

I feel myself and everything that has happened, everything I still haven't worked out about the revolution and Opantish and the coup, being put in a box and labeled "defeat." A cautionary tale, a sad news story.

Standing on the subway once, holding onto a metal pole, it takes me several minutes to realize that the music I'm hearing isn't in my head. It's coming out of the headphones of the young woman sitting nearby.

Zeedeeny ishqan zeedeeny
Ya ahla nawbat gonoony
(Make my passion grow
Oh, most beautiful fit of madness)

I look more closely at the source: inexpensive jeans, sneakers, a red jacket, hair shoulder-length, more straight than curly. Chipped silver polish on her fingernails, which are wrapped around the beat-up phone that's playing the music. I can see that the screen is lettered with Arabic script. This isn't someone who was born here, this isn't an Arab-American. This is someone who came here as an adult. The old world still clung to her, hovered in the air around her.

She is looking intently at the floor across from her, listening to this music. When the song ends, she starts it again, and she closes her eyes. The song is by Kazem al-Saher, the lyrics by the Syrian poet Nizar Qabbani. Kazem al-Saher, from Iraq, was called "the prince of love" when he exploded into mainstream popularity across the Arab world in the late '90s, putting Qabbani's clever, romantic poetry to melodies.

I'm not sure what I feel; whether I want to sit next to this girl in silence and listen to the song over and over again, until the train reaches the end of the line, or whether I want to get off the train and walk away quickly, taking large steps, comically outsized steps, and let the scene blend into the mesh of the city.

At Union Street, the woman stands up and gets off of the subway. I watch her walk down the platform, wonder if I should follow her, just to see where she goes, who she meets. Maybe we could be friends.

I stay put as the doors close and even when they momentarily reopen.

29

There is a border between any two bodies, of skin and perspective and the distances we hold around ourselves. We think that intimacy and meaning with others happens when these borders open up in patches. The distances grow smaller or vanish altogether, for a time, when we let someone in on our real thoughts, our real feelings, when we show them something that scared us.

There is a state where all of this protocol is suspended: in emergencies, in moments of danger, in situations where the individual is no longer supreme because survival depends on the ability to bond with others. You may stop knowing that you are opening, because that is now normal. When we are in a prolonged state of crisis, nothing is just mine or just yours.

But this state shouldn't be mistaken for complete fusion with others, with a total exchange. It is quieter than this. It is not that you understand me, or I you, because we are the same. There is simply no need to explain, to express, or to share, because there is an extraordinary leveling of the past, of the future. Between us, there is only now.

What happens when the crisis is over? How do we talk?

August 2015

By the time Farida moved to New York for graduate school, I'd lived in five different neighborhoods, bouncing from one sublet to another, sometimes with Omar when he was here, and sometimes on my own. I've learned that male roommates were almost always going to open the question but never asked, they would hide behind the silence of their communicated lust, cowardly boys in the bedroom next door, leaving me alone to deal with the discomfort, to harden to their gaze, to retreat from any shared activity. How else to refute their advance, which they left technically unmade?

Omar and I change the living room around to prepare for Farida's arrival. We move the two armchairs into the hallway, unroll the futon, bring a lamp in from my bedroom. The building sits on a corner of two wide avenues, and the apartment's two rooms each face a different street. It is too bright and too loud, and it feels like living in a glass box in the middle of the sidewalk. At night, there is the incessant passage of garbage trucks on their way to a plant, and before the trucks there are drunk young people roaming up and down the street, shouting about everything and nothing.

The building has a roof with views of the river that almost make up for the punishing interior. We sit up there after sunset, and it's calm. We ride bikes across the bridges, find somewhere to sit and have a drink. We talk, even in those first early days, of what she wants to create out of the years of revolution. Visual architecture—websites and archives and exhibitions—about the absurdity, the kitsch, the hollow faces of the state's deep dysfunction, its manic erasure of history.

"I want to work with you on something," she says. "Maybe like a collaborative journal—images and words. About this, about leaving and talking like this and being here."

A partnership begins to take shape in my mind, a new dimension in our friendship, and also the kind of collaboration that I've always wished to have the patience and generosity for. I buy a new notebook for our project. Red, with gold flecks on the soft leather cover. Spiral, with dotted lines on the pages.

But the next day Farida is cloudy. A black mood follows her around the apartment, out of the shower, to the coffeepot, back to her room. I try to gauge when to leave her alone and when to offer gentle invitations of tea, a snack. She accepts the tea but takes it into her room, says she's reading.

In the afternoon she asks if I want to go for a walk. It's overcast, and the air is warm and full, heavy. I imagine it could be punctured like a plastic bag full of water.

"Do you want an ice cream?" I ask.

"Yes, something with a lot of crap in it—M&Ms and cookies and all the sugariest, worst crap."

We stop in a deli, find the ice cream, and get a flavor with a silly name that promises a lot of crap. I suggest we walk to a little park by the water. It's small and inelegant, rimmed with a mesh fence on all sides except the river. The grass is scraggly and pale. There are a few groups of young white hippies who look like they are homeless by choice. We sit on a rock that might be artificial, near the water.

She stabs the ice cream with her plastic spoon, takes a few bites quickly, angrily, like she is pissed off at it, like she is punishing it by eating. I feel like I have to offer something.

"It's violent, leaving," I say. "We always think of it from the other side: we think about the people we leave behind, and all of the sadness seems to stay there. Even the phrase, 'leave behind,' it's like we built it so that the sadness is on that side. But it's also hard, once you've left, and I don't mean about adjusting and making new friends and whatever. You also have to deal with your own decision in a way that's very isolating."

Finally she says, "I don't know. I just feel like something is happening and I'll never be able to undo it. And I don't know what it is, and I don't know if it's good or bad, but it's this sort of alienation … not from here but from everything else, from before … like I'm alienated from myself."

November 2016

We stand outside a bar in the cold, smoking cigarettes, and Farida carefully tells me that she's angry with me. "But I'm over it, I just want to tell you because I don't want these things to stay quiet and fester between us."

She says I don't reciprocate in our friendship by opening up, by telling her when I'm bothered by things even as I'm still working through them. "I'm always coming to you when I'm upset or when I have a problem, but you never ever do, and there's something wrong in that imbalance."

It hits me then, with the clarity of self-recognition, that I have been playing this role of the supporter, a sort of older sister thing, although she had never really asked me to. Some of it came naturally from my being in New York first, but I had also probably been making up for what I could not offer her on the terrible night of her attack, for my loss of temper months later in the operation room. I had kept our friendship frozen in the shape of that night, and I needed to allow it to move on.

We finish our cigarettes and go inside. She is immediately at ease and herself with me, and I understand, then, that she has already thought a lot about this, and by the time she'd brought it up with me she had already decided we would move on. She had sensed that one or both of us, or our dynamic, couldn't handle a more raw or spontaneous confrontation.

The red notebook I had bought for the project with Farida eventually becomes a diary.

May 2016

There is the light of the end of the day, coming in the kitchen window and through the columns of the back of the blue chair across the table, just bought from a second-hand shop a few days ago. All of the other hours of the sun moving across the sky are just background, but that final hour, before it leaves, is an offering. It belongs to you.

This light does not seem appropriate for the word "dusk." It is less pink, yes, less dusky than the light in Cairo, which is filtered through the haze of pollution and kept distant, held on the horizon, pinks and oranges to be seen and admired. And isn't this what you came here for? For the cleaner air, for the sunset to seem like it could be yours?

You are reading Omar's book about the revolution, and not for the first time. But now you have to get up and pace around after certain passages, or stop the tears after the first few. Has your skin grown so thin? Have you become so weak in this place, with its need for clarity and the week's plans and your bank statement and your credit history?

But it is not about this place. It's about Cairo, polluted, pink-sunset Cairo, and the knowledge of what is gone, totally and completely gone.

What might be left for you there, now?

30

In the summer of 2016, I emailed T twice to see if she wanted to
meet for an interview. I had waited until I felt I couldn't wait any
longer, and I wasn't sure when I would be in Cairo again. She
didn't reply to my first email, but when I prodded, she wrote back
right away, said yes, of course, she would be happy to talk.

We agreed that I would come to her house in the late afternoon.
As I was leaving my apartment I stopped at the door, went back
into the kitchen, and took two mangoes from the fridge to take
with me.

As the cab pulled across Tahrir and into downtown, or maybe
it was later, as we stopped at the corner of her street, I realized: I
hadn't been to T's house since it stopped being the control room
three years earlier.

The thought slowed me down. I opened the taxi door and my
foot hovered above the street. I stood in front of the elevator for
a few moments before pressing the call button. I knew I would
go forward, but I needed to acknowledge the distance that I was
closing, or crossing, between now and then.

I stopped in front of her door, still covered in stickers of various protests and political groups, the yellow of the No Military Trials campaign popping out. Again I stood for a moment, unsure why, unsure what to think about or what to feel. I rang the doorbell, heard her footsteps come toward me. Then she, too, paused for a moment, before opening the door and letting me in with a smile.

The apartment looks entirely different—it's brighter and airier, even the furniture looks newer. We go into the kitchen to make tea, and she puts the mangoes in the fridge.

We bring our mugs into the living room. The beat-up old brown couch where I remember squeezing myself away from Farida is now tightly bound in buttery, pale yellow. It looks both clean and inviting.

"I feel that it's different talking with you than other people, even people highly involved, because we used your house, and so I feel like Opantish took over your life in this different way," I say after we sit down.

"I spent a long time unable to reconcile with the house … it was very traumatic. I still have the T-shirts, like 120 of them, and for a long time I had the flip charts and the rape kits and boxes full of I don't know what. It took years to reclaim the house. From the beginning of the revolution, the character of this place as a home was complicated, sometimes lost. There was no privacy, and back then I didn't mind people coming in and taking whatever they needed from the cupboard or sleeping in my bed or putting stickers on my wall, it was a communal space. To be honest, at the time it was a blessing. But now I'm much more private, more possessive."

She says she made changes around the apartment only recently, when work started coming in again, and she started buying, painting, up-cycling furniture from around the city. Lamps, chairs, even light fixtures she had been able to remold into her own.

I ask her if she talks about Opantish often. "Just yesterday I was talking about it—it's always there in one way or another. It's used as a point of reference, if you're reading about feminism or about organizing and power dynamics … aside from the nature of the thing we're doing, I mean the dynamics between us. It was the most complete form of organizing that happened in the revolution, in the sense that we had volunteers who we had *power* over.

"I don't know how we could have avoided it, given what we knew and where we were. But this power and the problems it created became very clear in calmer times, when we talked about what Opantish could do other than emergency response in the square. Should we work on Eid? Who's gonna be away, oh, all of the organizers. Let's vote, no let's revote because we don't like the result.

"At a certain point, we had to stop trying to make something out of it. What are we trying to preserve and why? Because we have a few hundred volunteers we don't want to lose?

"What connected people was the urgency—the hundreds of people that we thought of as some sort of endless resource—actually the only thing we have common is that we want women to not be raped … that's very thin as a common ground. And they were able to tolerate or be convinced that women needed to be on the ground."

We move out to her balcony to smoke. She says she stopped smoking indoors a while ago and also stopped smoking when she's alone. We sit at the small wooden table in a bit of shade. I'm surprised to see that "ACAB" (All Cops Are Bastards) is still spray-painted on the side of the next building over.

In the years after this interview, through writing about her own rape, through her work on ideas about consent in Egyptian cinema, T will continue to shape the discourse around sexual violence in Egypt. She will be a resource and a sounding board for many people, including myself, through several complicated moments in our postrevolution, post-#MeToo lives.

As T rolls a cigarette, she says she's still finding out about friends who had been assaulted in the square. "There was enough for it to happen to people close to you without your knowing. And, of course, there was the trauma of seeing people be both so changeable and also so overtaken. I don't think the people in the square in the eighteen days of 2011 that we romanticize so much were different from the people there two or two and a half years later," she says. "I just think the circumstances were different, just like the guy who had his finger up my ass was the same guy who a second later was protecting me and batting away the thief trying to steal my backpack."

This takes us to the night of her assault, being stuck in Shabrawy with three women, the ambulance afterward. She's ready to talk about it, she says. "Of course, I was never meant to be in the square that night or any night with Opantish, but I seemed to always end up there. If we could maintain these moments of high adrenaline with all their drama we'd be OK, but it's the aftermath where the crises happen. After January 25 I had PTSD and was drawing and healing for two or three months, and then there was the coup, and then after that I crashed again …

"One of the things we came out with, that we think of as a gain, is that we're agreed that 'survivor' is the politically correct term. But I'm not sure I necessarily prefer it to anything else. Because in a way when you're a survivor, this becomes part of you for the rest of your life. There's no way of forgetting it, it becomes part of your identity, you keep surviving, it's open-ended.

"Although 'survivor' is empowering, it strips some of the tragedy away. It almost makes me feel guilty for feeling like a victim, and getting better becomes my responsibility, but what if I can't get better? What if I am actually broken? Does it mean I'm not a good survivor? That I'm not doing what I'm supposed to?

"And we say it's the culture of blaming the victim, but we don't call it the culture of blaming the survivor. When am I a victim and when am I a survivor?"

T: Facebook, November 2016

Arwa, I promised you I would write today. For a month now, every time we talk we find ourselves in a bind that we cannot solve. You push me to remember and I resist. I don't want to remember, you go over the details with me, you ask me to confirm to you that this happened, that you are not crazy.

No, Arwa, you are not crazy. This happened. To you and to me and to them.

Yes, Arwa, our friends, our comrades, comrades in the revolution remember Mohamed Mahmoud every year around this time with nostalgia and masochism, they build walls for the heroes who were injured and killed, they remember even the small children that used to break up rocks, they write poems, but they do not remember us … we are nothing, we are "what made you go there, we are collateral damage the women who were assaulted and the women who resisted and went down after they were assaulted so that they would not be defeated, to defend other women, even the men who were beaten and hurt with us, all of these are roles/heroes that mean nothing to them.

Arwa I know you are angry and defeated, but I have passed the stages of anger and defeat, I am disgusted and bored and I don't have the faith to be angry, this is the end of them. We were stupid and romantic, we thought that people who went out against power and defeated it would definitely go out against all injustice, that people who called for freedom must believe in freedom for everybody, but it turned out that that's not necessarily true, Arwa ... turns out it's normal to be both revolutionary and patriarchal ... that someone against military rule can also be a harasser ... that someone against the brotherhood can also believe we should stay home so that we don't distract them with our side problems and they can focus on "the battle."

Maybe these are the only people that I can think of and call "we." I do not regret it, Arwa, and I will not hesitate to do this again and again, the only difference will be that next time I'll know that I don't need to expect anything from a lot of people, that there is a small group which will stand with me and I am always grateful for that, grateful that they exist and that they are crazy, like us, and will go out to combat the revolving masses with their bodies.

Arwa: Facebook, November 2016

The only event that I was sure I had overcome in its moment now wakes me up, years later. "What happened?"

I don't wake up because of the memory, I wake up out of anger, I want to remember but I cannot.

"Tell me what happened, I don't remember."

This has become a routine phone call to my friend.

"When was it, do you remember when it was?"

We begin a search, her and I, to discover the date of the event, I go back and listen to what I said on TV programs and what I wrote, I hear my voice and I feel that this was a different person, completely far away from me. Why was I so calm?

I go back and remember, I was calm because what pained me was not the event I was talking about. What pained me was the feeling that we were alone, in the middle of a popular revolution. It was the silence, the denial, and in the best case the avoidance/willful ignorance.

I am writing for the fourth year and every year I feel that I am trying to breathe life into a dead body that no one wants to remember, except a very few.

It is a deadly feeling of loneliness, from all that has happened to us. The victory is collective and the dream is collective but the defeat, even if temporary, will remain personal no matter how much we share it.

After reading her post, I watch a video of Arwa on Lamees al-Hadidy's talk show from 2013. I don't know why or how I didn't watch this back when it aired, a few days after Yasmine El-Baramawy's interview, after that terrible January 25.

Arwa wears a green jacket, and her hair is in a bob. Her glasses are square, dark-rimmed. A notepad in front of her, a pen in her hand. She looks sharp.

She speaks with energy and clarity. She tells the hostess, a woman who is now aligned with the new military regime, what happened to her. How she saw a woman being attacked and, when she intervened, she became the target herself. She describes the hands and nails and words without pause. Like Yasmine, there is no anger in her voice, no fear.

There is more heat when she talks about the state's complicity, about Black Wednesday in 2005 when their thugs surrounded women protesters, stripped them of their clothes. These attacks, Arwa says, are attacks not only on women as women, they are on women as revolutionaries, as protesters, as citizens.

Across the table from her is Jeannette, who had also been with a makeshift patrol unit. Arwa says she wouldn't have made it out without Jeannette's help. Jeannette is looking down at the table between them. She looks like she might cry.

When Jeannette speaks she says that she held on to Arwa for about twenty minutes in the mob, that what she was most worried about was that Arwa would faint and fall. "Then I'd lose her, I wouldn't be able to get her up, there would be trampling."

She says, "I'll admit this, I had an electric taser with me, and it was the only thing that was useful."

As Jeannette speaks, Arwa looks at her with a small sideways smile. She seems so together, so assertive. I know that Arwa is not OK anymore. I know she is struggling. I haven't seen her in a long time, but I hear this from friends. I think about her and I send her emails that feel inarticulate, insufficient.

31

Interview: Yasmine El-Baramawy, 2016

I find Yasmine at a concert she gave, her first in years. When I show up, she's rehearsing at the back, discussing the lineup with the tabla player who would accompany her. I catch a glimpse of her smoking a cigarette, greeting someone.

They start about fifteen minutes late. She sits in front of a graffiti-covered wall, facing an audience sitting on cushions on the floor. The tabla player sits to her left. Between them is an easy friendliness.

At the end of the concert, she says, "I'll wrap up with another one of my own songs, named for my friend Arwa."

We meet a few days later in a coffee shop. She has a soft voice and a steady gaze. Her hair is still long, all the way down her back, and it's got some gray in it now.

She tells me that a few months after she went on TV and her friend yelled at her and called her a bitch in their living room, she began to see something else behind his anger. When she said, "They raped me, dozens of them, in front of everyone," he understood that it wasn't that some number of men had crossed over, eyes wide open, to an unforgivable place. That place could not hold them, their harm and what it meant. Because what she was saying was: these are our people, they exist in the revolution and outside of it, we say we are here for ideals but we are only as good as the people standing next to us in the fight.

So what does their transformation into vessels of violence say about us? What are we going to do about it? What are *you* going to do?

For a year after the attack, Yasmine was constantly being interviewed. European and American news and documentary crews would come to her house, sit in the living room, and tape. They filmed her when she went with the lawyers to file a suit against the government and its law enforcement agencies under the Rome Statute, which holds states accountable for mass crimes.

After nearly every interview, a member of the crew—the cameraman, the producer, the journalist herself—stayed behind, sometimes just a few seconds, to tell Yasmine that they had also been raped or abused. As the rest of the team waited by the elevator, they would tell her and say, "I just wanted you to know that."

She started trying to guess, during the interviews, which one of them it would be.

She sometimes calls the attack "the accident," the same word you would use for a car crash, which is also what Habiba called the whole revolution once.

"I found a year had gone by, and I had stopped playing music. I was constantly talking about the accident."

Circling around the attack allowed her to believe she had somehow moved past it. She had become branded as a sort of spokesperson on sexual violence and, whenever a story was in the news, the media called her automatically. "We need a victim," they'd say to her. But what did she have to say about sexual harassment on campus, when all anyone saw when they looked at her was gang rape in Tahrir?

Then on the one-year anniversary of her attack, November 23, 2013, she had a full panic attack, and when she was able to breathe again, she understood that she hadn't dealt with what had happened to her. The crews, the talking, the lawsuit were focused on getting a reaction from the public. She was obsessed with what people were going to do in response, with what they weren't doing.

She stopped doing the interviews. In the stillness, the new emptiness of her time, she found she was alone.

She had lost Nadia, Nadia who had been her closest friend.

"She was my person ... I couldn't talk without her, but when she was there I would open up, find what I had to say. I couldn't feel anything, I couldn't even cry, except with her." When she says "with her" she doesn't use *ma'aha*, which you would you use to say, for example, I went to the store "with" someone. She uses *beeha*, which is used for tea with sugar, or pregnant with twins. Its meaning stretches beyond companionship.

Nadia who was there when the attack started, Nadia who was pulled away from her, surrounded by another group of men, dragged across the square to the alley of a fast-food restaurant. Nadia who had fought her way out, saved herself by turning her body into wood and using a psychological power that she didn't know she had available to her, appealing to the men around her to save her, calling them her heroes. She saved her body for her life and for her son. Nadia who, after she was rescued by a group of friends and strangers who took her up to T's apartment, kept saying, "Yasmine, Yasmine."

Imagine this.

Nadia who came back to her in the mob, and Yasmine's shirt was gone, her bra was gone, and Nadia hugged her, and *can you imagine this?* the mob tried to pull them apart again.

A month later, they were supposed to go on television together. Nadia changed her mind the day before. "I can't do this to my family," she said.

Afterward, she started distancing herself from Yasmine. She started dismissing what Yasmine was doing, saying things like: "Yasmine has time to go to do all these interviews. I couldn't do it, I have to work."

A couple of months after the TV appearance, she came to Yasmine to end their friendship. She said that it was nothing that Yasmine had done, though she knew she'd been mean to her. She just couldn't be around her, it was too painful.

Yasmine thinks she understands what Nadia meant. There were people who came to her in friendship, support, love, and for some reason she needed them to disappear right away. Not walk away, not leave and shut the door behind them, just turn into smoke or air. Negated. Deleted. As though they had never been flesh. It was never because of anything they had done. It was like an inevitable chemistry, one she couldn't alter. To carry on being around them would be like standing in front of an air conditioner on full blast, in soaking wet clothes, and trying not to shiver.

"When she's ready, I will still be her friend," Yasmine said.

"You know, sometimes I go to European cities and I see the memorials they built for war crimes, for the horrible things they have done to one another on that continent. And I think that those structures are about a society's shame, and I think that's why there are no memorials for mass rape. It's as though it can't be treated as the heinous crime against humans that it is. It is either relegated to the realm of monstrosity, of evil that cannot be explained and therefore cannot be confronted, or it is dismissed, diminished, removed from the conversation."

She left the center of the city and moved to one of its most distant suburbs, skipping over all the orbits in between. If she was going to continue to circle around this thing, she would do it from the greatest distance possible, and maybe this way it wouldn't sneak up on her so often. Maybe this way she would see it coming.

Even the building she moved into was on the outer ring of this new development. The view from her bedroom was westward, toward a desert that wasn't exactly open because there were a few construction sites nearby, but nothing high had been built up. Here, she could be as alone as she felt she was already.

She says to me, "I would sit on the floor, facing a corner of the room. I would play a note, just one note ... *tinnnnn*. I would sit and listen until after its sound had gone, after the ring had left and come back to me." She is smiling. "Then I would do it again. I could do this for three hours at a time. Just sit, with just one note."

32

January 2017

We are standing in the kitchen at a party near downtown Cairo, talking about coming back to the city and leaving it, the choice that hangs over the heads of those lucky enough to have it. Every day, a choice.

The lights are off, the illumination comes in from above the bar that connects the kitchen to the spacious living room. There, red lights, and people dressed mostly in black, mostly sitting down, mostly talking quietly. They seem to be on a drug that we haven't been offered. We don't know anyone here. This is a younger scene. The hostess has short curly hair—don't we all—and all I know of her is her name, that she is queer, and that many of her gatherings feature various states of nudity. A friend tells me she once turned up at one of these parties and was let into the apartment by a man wearing nothing but a bowtie.

I think I understand this, understand the need for it like water in a city where every square inch of public space is policed by cops, honorable citizens, or lechers.

Outdoors, we find our masks: stern and unsmiling, or sweet and female. We neutralize ourselves, make ourselves inconspicuous. We become locked into a battle with our own bodies, flattening them, hiding them. Invisibility becomes the only achievable victory outside closed doors. I remember once regretting wearing the color red.

So the walls grow thicker. The distance between indoors and outdoors grows greater and more critical.

A guy comes up to me holding his phone, asks if I want to put a beer order in. It's a dry night, in honor of the prophet's birthday, but everyone has a phone number to work around this. I say no, thank you, I'm leaving soon.

Arwa is standing by the kitchen sink, which she's tipping her cigarette ash into. She's looking out the window, her back to us. I think twice before approaching her.

"What's going on? Are you alright?"

"I'm fine, fine. What are you up to? How long are you staying?" she asks, turning toward me.

"I'm here for a couple of months at least. I'm working on the book I told you about. I'm also just happy to be here and not be in a rush, you know?"

She exhales, pushing the smoke away from me with her free hand. For some reason this prompts me to ask her for a cigarette. She still smokes L&Ms, the blue ones.

"I think it's really good you're writing," she says.

I tell her that I read her Facebook post and that it moved me.

"It's horrible, it's a horrible feeling, not owning your story, somehow not knowing it," she says.

"Tell me about it," I say, and try not to end with a question mark in my voice.

"Do you actually, really want to know?"

She says she had lost her mind and only recently found her way back to it.

"OCD," she says. "It turns out there are all these different ways it can look—it's not always about counting and symmetry. It's about obsessive thoughts that take over, internally. The external bit is the compulsive behavior, and that can be a lot of different things."

She talks about therapy, about how much better things started to feel once she had been diagnosed but how hard it still was sometimes. They think, she and her therapist, that the OCD was triggered by the assault and by the rupture in her personal life afterwards, the breakup of a long-term relationship.

She's moved closer to me now, or we've moved closer to each other, and the air around our bodies seems to tell everyone else to leave us alone. She is drinking a club soda. I have the dregs of a beer.

"You know what happened, with him, right?" she asks, meaning her ex-boyfriend, and of course I know. I remember seeing her after they broke up, and I also remember because she put his words in the middle of what she wrote then, and they burned like the bright center of her anger.

His words fell on me like bullets:
"You wanted this to happen to you so you wouldn't feel guilty about the other girls."

She speaks more about betrayal. "We were completely on our own. And now nobody wants to remember."

She is holding calmness in her face as she speaks. But if her anger took physical form it would be hot like bubbling wax, and it would stick to your skin, making sure you wouldn't forget it.

I search for something to say and end up with a series of questions—how will we deal with this, this silence about the battle that was at the heart of the war, that became the war itself, that turned us toward each other? There are no answers to my questions, and we both know that.

When we move toward our friends and she keeps an arm around me, I worry that I have failed—that what she wants is someone to listen, not to share or join her. That I have somehow become another person for her to comfort.

I decide that this cannot be so—that we have to keep an eye on the line between solidarity and freezing someone in a state of victimhood. I am here now, and I will need this line, this way out.

33

Nahya and I are sitting across from each other in the Korean restaurant. We stopped eating an hour ago, but I haven't seen her since I've been back, and there's a lot to talk about. Things are softer and more open between us now. She's thinking about going abroad for a while, and I feel less judged by her.

"Three of you have the same name," I say. "So you'd better tell me a name that you'd like me to use for you in the book."

She thinks.

"Call me Nahya," she says. My mind starts to break it down for its meaning. Nahya: the preventor. The person who ends things, who is the ending. It's also the name of a working-class neighborhood in Cairo.

"I like the neighborhood. You know, back in 2005, Nahya was where the youth group in the Kifaya [Enough] movement went when we broke away from the old leadership and started taking action on our own. That's where we met for our very first anti-government protest."

It flashes through my mind: we are still in university. I don't really know her yet, she is dating a friend of mine, and we all get together in the early evening. She shows up straight from the protest with dusty trousers and bright eyes.

"I've never been to Nahya," I say. I know a journalist from there who was imprisoned for two years. He told me that the cops hate his neighborhood because people there are poor and defiant.

"I like the meaning, too," she says. "And I think I have a bit of this in my personality: to sort of stop people from doing things. To be a killjoy." She smiles.

"You're not a killjoy," I say, and I mean it. She is my encouraging friend. I think of forward motion when I think of her. "I like the sound of the name, it's pretty," I say.

"It's the name I want to call my daughter, if I have one," she says.

We've been thinking about kids. Nahya is certain she wants to have at least one in a couple of years, after she's had some more time to study, to get back into theatre work.

"You have an olive in your belly!" she says as we walk out of the restaurant.

"Isn't it weird that everyone we know is having boys?" I say.

"You'll have to protect him in a totally different way," she says. "It's OK, we'll all help you."

I'm about five months pregnant when Omar and I move back. We'd already been craving more open-ended time in Cairo, and we wanted to have the baby near family, within a community we still feel part of.

I swim in the private club we have inherited access to. I keep my head underwater, listen to the faraway chatter of people sunning themselves. I wonder whether this is what the world sounds like to the baby, and whether he feels a double buoyancy when we are in the pool. I read that he is often still when I move, because my motion puts him to sleep. I imagine him in there, comfortably suspended as I glide us through the water.

Getting dressed afterward, I see drops of breast milk for the first time.

I had navigated adulthood without thinking very much about the question of having children or imagining what life would be like as a mother. I'd read and thought much more about the social and political consequences of women choosing to be childless than I had about the politics around childbirth itself, even though I had no strong feelings about it either way.

When I am pregnant, I am desperate for information and for the company of other women, especially those who had been pregnant before. I don't have many around me, and so my search for literature becomes even more intense. I read Maggie Nelson and Iman Mersal and Dorothy Dinnerstein. I say that pregnancy and birth are underrepresented as human experiences. Over time I start to wonder if this is really true, or if the stories and questions are there and I had ignored them, thought them unimportant, banal.

The duality of pregnancy as both an everyday occurrence and a drawing board for societal and existential polarities plays out in my body. The veins on the back of my hands stick out like windy, greenish-blue rubber tracks, and I learn that I'm making about one and a half times more blood than usual. My waist is disappearing, an expected distortion that makes me wonder when exactly it is that I start becoming more than myself. Is it when I start taking extra vitamins? When I start avoiding car fumes not for my own breathing lungs but for the new ones that I (I?) am still forming? When I feel a kick, see a face scanned onto a screen that looks ghostly but human? In some sense, my body has always been treated like it was not just mine—it was always all of its reproductive potential, both a potential asset and a potential disruption.

Birth is scary and unknown to me, unreasonable on its surface.
How will we separate? No one knows exactly what triggers labor,
but they think the baby sends a hormonal signal that starts the
process. I learn that labor comes in stages and that by the end, the
baby's head is tucked down into its chest so that the smallest part
of its skull is what makes its way through the birth canal. My mind
blows open. I try to keep it that way—open—to what's coming.

I want to give my body a chance to see this thing through, this
sophisticated and creative act that it was doing with a will that was
completely independent from my conscious mind. I want to work
with it to see what the climax of this process feels like.

Some of the natural birth literature I read feels dogmatic,
making it seem as though we should all not only be capable of
drug-free births but even come to *enjoy* labor. But at its core, the
approach works off the idea that given enough information and
support, women can manage the pain of labor and, in most cases,
deliver more healthily without medical intervention.

My first doctor doesn't think I can handle it. "You can try," he
said to me when I was six months pregnant, buttoning my blouse
back up around my belly on the exam table. "But it's the second
most painful thing you can go through, after total body burn." *But
how do you know?* I thought.

Once I start talking to other women about this, the stories of a
healthcare system that treats us as passive clients don't stop. One
woman tells me that, during a scan, her doctor refused to tell her
the baby's estimated weight. "If I give you a number, will it mean
anything to you?" he said.

Maternal and infant mortality are low in Egypt because birth is
heavily medicalized, but that also means that the rates of unneces-
sary cesarean sections is one of the highest in the world. Cesareans
can be life-saving operations when they're needed. They are also

a major surgery that carries medical risks, a long recovery period, and a proven increase in rates of postpartum depression. Elective C-sections became so normalized women asked one another "When's your operation?" rather than "When is the baby due?"

Pregnant and writing this book, I find myself living a connection that I had only scratched at before. That something about cultures of contempt for women, of refusal to see them as equal in systems that are set up by men, rotates around this biological difference that makes us able to deliver life. That it—we—need to be controlled because we have this ability, which makes us so powerful but also, at times, so vulnerable. That we need to be defined by it.

The bodily fights in Tahrir and our choices about whether and how to give birth, and how we're treated for those choices within institutions like medicine, workplaces, and families, are connected by a politics of sexual control that manifests far beyond Egypt. As I write this, women's right to choose whether to carry a pregnancy is under renewed threat in the United States, a place where that right has already been severely diminished. The US version of healthcare also means that the maternal mortality rate is higher than any other developed country and that a Black woman's chances of dying while carrying or delivering life is three times that of a white woman. Everything about this—about childbirth—is political, has always been political.

34

It's in the night, specifically in the hour before sunrise, that the unborn baby is most active, turning and kicking. By my/his eighth month he is kicking me awake with one foot, the other lodged underneath my right ribcage.

I used to work in the predawn hours. I started doing this in college, with nearly due research papers, and then later, as I wrote parts of this book around a full-time job, setting my alarm for 4:00 a.m. I kept at it while pregnant, working through sunrise when insomnia woke me up. But as the quality of my sleep disappeared despite the maternity pillow and the relaxing teas, I realized that I was no longer awake by choice. I was awake because I was huge and could not get comfortable, and because the baby was exercising, pushing my insides outward, bumping into the edges of his temporary world.

In those last weeks during which he is folded inside my skin, I struggle to think of anything else. When he kicks me out of bed I read about breastfeeding, about the mental development of newborns.

Through childbirth, people I love are there with me and they help make it happen, holding me up and putting pressure on my hips and passing me a bucket to throw up in and shooing nurses and fetal monitors away for many long hours through the night. They are part of my labor. But at some point, when I've stopped counting the hours, when I no longer know what time is, they are very far away, their voices distant. My water still has not broken, and it feels like there is a planet inside of me that wants to explode. It is angry and shaking and it is a planet that is full of oceans and it pushes out against my barriers and it wants to erupt. The doctor offers to break the waters and I say yes, please, and the relief is warmth running down my thighs.

The room is full of people, but I am alone; I am alone with the baby who wants to be born. We are both in distress and we need each other to get out of our predicament. There is nothing anyone can do. I move and squat and crouch on my knees. I call out for my mother. They convince me to get on my back to measure the baby's heart rate and Omar has to hold me up and half-carry me. I can't move my limbs, I want to be on the floor on all fours, I can feel how enormous my heaviness is against him as he tries to heave me up unto the bed and when I get on my back it's excruciating but the contractions are slowing down, they say. I've been through the long part, the part of irregular contractions that are still building, I am now in the heart of the fight, the bloody pit at the center of it all, I am ready to push this baby out and the urge overtakes me like automation and I get on all fours on the bed and I say "I want to push" and I begin pushing and I remember, I understand that pushing means the end is near but the hospital staff have decided they need to move me to an operating room but I want to push. Get on your back they say, no I'm not moving I say, so they wheel me out on all fours and they are aghast at the sight of me in public, my robe hanging open, breasts and blood visible to everyone.

In the operating room bright lights and surgical masks and sudden authority and I am not sure about this and they say you have to get on your back so we can deliver this baby but I need to push I say and they say things about heart rates and contractions and the baby's heart that beat so loud and so fast when we first heard it seven months ago, *how can something so small already have a heart,* and so I say OK and I lie on my back and I am pushing but I feel like I am late, like I am in a test now under these bright lights and I am pushing but it doesn't feel the same, the pull of the earth underneath me is gone, I'm going the wrong way. The doctor says he will have to do a small cut to help the baby's head get out, he will give me a local anesthetic, but I can't imagine that I will feel anything there ever again. I say OK and then I still need to push, push hard, he says, we need the baby's head out with this one and I think I have a little bit left, I imagine it's like the last Tic Tac in a box of Tic Tacs, that's how much I have left and I put it all in that push. After this tucked-in head, the rest comes easy.

And then on my chest, to my deepest astonishment, is the baby, blue and crying and looking although he cannot see yet. A new planet, a new center of gravity.

35

We tried, Omar and I, to be partners in parenting from the beginning, to allow our child to form multiple attachments, to feel secure with and close to his father, ultimately to encourage him to have freer, healthier ideas about gender and intimacy. We rolled up our sleeves and got ready for pumping and storing breast milk, for sharing night shifts. We'd always been good as a team.

As I breastfed, Omar put water down in front of me before I realized I was thirsty; periodically, he forced me to go to bed and shut the door with the baby in his arms, not opening it again until I'd slept for nine hours. I would wake up feeling like my edges had been smoothed, except for my breasts, which would be hard and leaking. Our connection with one another felt strong like steel, like it would withstand this enormous change.

For the first few months of the baby's life, he kept all other commitments to a minimum, but there was an unavoidable ten-day trip to France for his novel about the revolution. In my journal, a list of things I learn cannot be done with one hand:

Make coffee
Peel an orange
Write a thoughtful email

And things that can:

Make a cheese sandwich
Start a load of laundry
Shave legs

Sometime in that first year of parenthood, once the euphoria of the newness of a new life had waned, everything between us started to fray. A previously invisible architecture was making itself shown, and we found ourselves in one of modernity's oldest stories, surprising only because of how insidious it turned out to be.

Ideas and attitudes—some that I'd suppressed and others that I'd thought I'd rejected—were pulled to the surface as we tried to share the work of taking care of a baby and remain reasonably put-together human beings living in a reasonable domestic space. The amount of labor needed to maintain daily life increased exponentially: laundry, cleaning, thinking about food. More often than not I'd rush to do things first, because somewhere in my brain it was deeply impressed on me that this was how it was done. I had not seen men doing housework before, not real housework. Not keeping a constant mental stock of what is in the fridge and what needed resupplying, not thinking to wash the curtains once a year, not knowing how to store winter blankets so they were safe from moths. Between us I was the one who was given tips and skills on keeping house, and, whether or not I had paid attention or thought they were important at the time, here they were, being relevant, and I was rushing to achieve some supercharged version of female domestic competence that I had thus far been entirely uninterested in. "Stop doing the laundry," Omar said one afternoon, and for a few days we each sort of rushed to get to the machine first. Trying to parent equally became—and remains—an act of constant rebalancing.

Since I was the one breastfeeding, it was always easier, faster for me to go to the baby. So I did, carried through by hormones and adrenaline that kept me functional until they didn't. We were both tired, but—much more frequently, almost consistently—I was exhausted. I envied Omar's ability for clear thought, his ability to write when I could barely read.

I began to feel a particular kind of loneliness, one to which I could see no end. None of our close friends in Cairo had children, and my own mother was away. Friends stepped in as best as they knew how to, but what I needed was someone who had been there, who had been through the extended gray-black, the long bruise of this change.

The fights between Omar and me in this period were horrible, for the first time since we'd known each other. Our expectations and disappointments in each other were fresh and raw and frightening. We needed to grow larger. Our connection needed to bend and breathe; steel was no good here.

I had thought, had hoped, that I would finish writing this book before giving birth. I didn't manage to do this, and when I tried to return to it a few months into the baby's life I felt late, like the book was overdue for some invisible jury, and every time I sat with it I was overtaken by a rush of thoughts, my brain wild with sleeplessness.

I write:

Time is running out.

Tasks are mapped out, a sequence—play meal clean nap—that repeats itself every hour or two. I am running on adrenaline.

It's not just time that's coming at me from all sides.

I have spun loops of memory and narration that have grown thick and tangled around me and now I feel stuck, wrapped in the vines and branches that I have planted.

No one has asked me to write this story. I could just leave it as a painful history, to be examined only periodically, personally.

But:

I am real, it says. You were there. The same you who is now a stroller-pushing mom who hasn't read the news in three weeks, you were there with a group of radical women who fought with their bodies and their tongues.

36

July 2019

There is no air on the train. It's moving fast and deep across South London, and we're below ground that has rarely been hotter. The carriage empties out as we go farther and farther east.

A man wearing shorts and a T-shirt, his hair in long dreadlocks down his back, stands at the open window at the top of the car, catching the harsh underground breeze that the train makes. I look at the backs of his legs, covered in skull tattoos. I try to remember the last time I saw M.

When I first met her, about a year before Opantish and the attacks, she was still living as a man most of the time. She was living in Cairo, working on energy policy for a progressive NGO.

In my memory she wore a lot of muted colors—beige, light gray—and had a quick smile and a habit of bending toward you across a table when she laughed.

I haven't seen her since she started living consistently as a woman. I have seen photos of her with small breasts under her T-shirt. I've followed some of her ongoing work on energy and climate change. We tried to do this interview over Skype a few years back, but it didn't work out, and once I heard that she was transitioning I felt that I wanted to be with her when we spoke about this.

I get out of the station, anxious for fresh air, and it's a perfect, long, early summer evening. Her house is still a bus ride away. As we move down the high street, I see a group of friends walking down the pavement, pink hair, blue hair. M lives in a multiparent household, and I know that there a few young kids. She herself is expecting a baby with her partner, who is carrying it.

We're turned off the high street now. Chicken shops, a funeral parlor.

I get out and walk down her street, a narrow one with neat rows of Victorian houses, and I am having a hard time imagining visibly queer parents walking around this neighborhood. I don't know how much of this is conditioning from Cairo, from the built-in reflex to hide.

She answers the door slightly breathless, hugs me, and rushes me back to the kitchen, which leads out to the back garden, where the party is. She makes a new batch of some kind of cocktail as kids zoom past our legs.

We step outside and a small boy drops his popsicle on the grass. "Do you want me to lick it clean for you?" she asks him, and somehow this makes me relax.

Inevitably, I spend a long time speaking to the other Arab woman there. She and I and M are standing together when she asks me about this book and what it's about. I start explaining about Opantish, and M's face darkens slightly. She looks away and steps back, leaves us a while.

She had already agreed to the interview, so I knew she wasn't opposed to the project or to talking with me about it. But when we meet up a week later at a café near her house for our sit-down, she says that she doesn't like talking about it with people in London, or with people who aren't already very familiar with what had happened, because of how persistent the racialized tropes around Arab men are.

She had arrived in Cairo in 2011, at the beginning of her trip toward transitioning, as she calls it, and began presenting herself as a woman whenever she was back in London. "I knew I was queer, and I knew I was on a direction, and on my first visit back to London from Cairo I started presenting as myself consistently." Then it would be back to Cairo and presenting as a man, although she would often get teased or harassed on the metro with *ya wad ya bit* (roughly: hey boy hey girl).

"There were little pockets, little moments, like I remember being at the beach in Sinai and linking up with N and putting nail polish on, and wearing skirts on the beach and feeling like, oh this is fine. Then, of course, I went back to Cairo, and I forgot to take the nail polish off and I was walking around with my hands in my pockets and feeling like, *oh shit*."

"The switching back and forth was definitely a head fuck," she says. "Especially when it came to Opantish. There was one point at which I was the only one who could reach a woman, and I got her out on my own. I was being groped and the rest of it, but it would have been so much worse if I'd been presenting as a woman. I wouldn't have been able to get us out of there."

It becomes clear, as she's speaking, that she's talking about the attack on Nora, when she was cut with a knife between her legs. "I remember standing there and having to choose between the group of people who were assaulting her worse but moving in the right direction, and those who were being less harmful but going in the wrong direction. I had to choose between letting her top go or her trousers. I had to let her top go."

"These choices ... ," she says.

The heaviness is down on us now; she has lowered her cheek onto the crook of her arm, extended across the table. We're quiet for a few moments.

"I left Cairo so much more physically violent than I had been when I arrived. We had to be so violent in Opantish, it was something a few of the men in particular talked about. This kind of dismantling of our boundaries around violence ... I used to take the metro every day, and I would often intervene if someone was bothering a woman, or sometimes when people would bother me with saying *ya wad ya bit* or whatever. But one day some guy was bothering a woman, and straight away I just threw him against a wall, and I thought, OK, something's going on here."

She'd already had experience using her body in confrontations with riot police. In the United States, in Palestine, in England. But she'd never been in anything like this—where the people you were fighting were ostensibly the same people who were in your revolution, not uniformed, not identifiable.

"I've spent a lot of time letting myself move on from it," she says. "I moved to London, and I decided: I'm going to make a home here."

Soon after, she stopped presenting as a man altogether. "You know some friends from Cairo think that it's because of Opantish that I became a woman," she says, laughing, annoyance at the edge of her voice.

We move to a pub nearby and talk some more. I've switched off my recorder. We talk about our exes and the people we still have in common, share notes on those we've lost touch with. She hasn't been back to Cairo since she left, and she doesn't plan to. She had moved there to work with the revolution, and she got involved—

really involved. When the time for that was over, she moved on. There is no nostalgia or romance in her conversation.

We talk about motherhood, and the baby her partner is carrying, made with M's sperm. M is planning to breastfeed, her partner is still not sure she'll do the same. M has taken a combination of drugs—some of which she was taking before the pregnancy—to be able to do this. She is, she says, already lactating.

I am trying not to seem too awestruck. I didn't think breastfeeding could be constructed by us in this way. The whole thing had rushed through my body just because I'd let it, a hormonal sequence that changed my systems and synchronized itself with the baby. Here was M, taking hormones that brought her closer to her partner's state during pregnancy, already lactating and pumping. It blows my mind.

"You know, if you decided to have another baby, Omar could do this, too," she said.

I don't need this trans-ability in the same way. But I know, selfishly, that even if I don't need it myself, other people having it and doing it will make my femaleness easier, less sacred. Freer.

37

At a springtime barbeque, when I'm nearly done working on this book, Adam tells me that part of what helped Opantish work so much better after the January 25 anniversary attacks was a new technique we started using for scouting. "Instead of scouts roaming the square, they—and they were usually these young, lithe guys—would climb to a viewpoint high above ground, like a lamppost," Adam says.

There would be four or five of them in different parts of the square and they would scan the crowds, looking for attacks. "They would call us on the phones or run up and tell us: *it's happening here*, or *it's moved over there*. They could see what we couldn't. We called them the 'birds.'"

At many points while writing and revising this book, I've longed for that distant viewpoint, for release from the details of this history. I feel this when the story seems impossible to tell, when I've spent too long on my own with the changing pages of the text, working around a violence that repeats itself, in different ways, over and over again around me as time moves on. Sometimes what leads me out of my trap is a conversation, but more often I go back and listen to an interview, and something—a detail, an insight, a joke—pulls me out.

Toward the end of most interviews, a slight wariness makes itself heard in people's voices. These conversations, these re-openings, are a kind of labor. I hear the nervousness that vibrates in my voice when I'm speaking with women. It's not there when I'm speaking with men. What is that? Am I automatically on firmer ground with men—because I'm somehow more naturally entitled to be a part of this than they are? Do I feel more apologetic with women? Does this nervousness that I think I hear also carry guilt?

For a long time, my guilt was a silent companion while I wrote. I knew that it was there—I must have known, I alluded to it in an essay I wrote before I began the very first draft of this book, where I wrote that *we felt guilty for the survival of our flesh*. I knew that I felt *badly* for being spared what others had not. But I did not dwell on or investigate this feeling. I didn't think I needed to. It was random, this luck, but retrospection laces it with questions about whether I'd gone to the front lines enough, been brave enough.

They say that survivors of secondary traumas sometimes become obsessed with the violence they were spared, that they keep coming back to it. I don't think that's what happened here. But I did feel some responsibility, some sense that since I wasn't physically assaulted the way so many were, the least I could do was put my writing toward telling some version of the story. As though the psychological cost of that was not penance, exactly, but something I could more reasonably be asked to afford.

I knew, also, that I could not write anything else until I had written this.

38

January 2016

The silence between Farida and me about what happened to her cracks open on a night in New York, in the dead of winter. We're in a part of the city we rarely go, to see an art show. I wait for her under an awning outside the museum as snow falls sideways, millions of flakes barely heavier than air but with a cumulative effect so disruptive that it has stopped airplanes and trains.

She shows up wearing a black leather jacket, not nearly warm enough, and red lipstick. She can pull this rock-and-roll chic off better than anyone I know.

The show has taken over the entire museum. The building used to be a public school, and the hallways are long, with big windows that fill them with white sunlight. The rooms that open to the right and left hold work by different artists about New York and their experiences of how the city has changed.

One piece, by an older man, is a photograph of a tunnel in Central Park which had been a free love alleyway in the '60s and '70s. The sex of the place has been wiped away like so much of what nostalgia identifies as a grittier, freer city. The artist painted over the picture with a reddish copperlike metallic paint, until it was almost monochromatic, and then projected the piece onto the wall in front of me.

This is the only piece in the show that I return to. What matters is not that the tunnel has changed. It's the paint over the photograph, the light projecting it onto the wall: the piece is about what *he* had done to the tunnel, because of, or for, his memory.

After walking through most of the rooms, we find a Japanese restaurant nearby and eat food strange enough to balance out the banality of seeing a terrible art show.

"How's the writing going?" Farida asks.

"I still need to do more interviews—next time I'm in Cairo."

"Are you writing to specific people or doing a wider call?"

"I'm writing to specific people, mostly people who were in the organizing team."

I pause for a minute, pick at the label on my beer.

"I'm afraid to write to certain people," I say. "I'm afraid I'll retraumatize them. You know, stir the old wounds."

"No, you can't let that stop you," she says, shaking her head. "It will be so much more hurtful if the book comes out and they don't see their voices in it. Just write to them, and at least then they've had the choice, they've been asked."

"You're right, I know you're right," I said.

Then she says, "You know, I can barely remember my attack. I've blocked it out, almost completely."

I am stunned.

Farida is a fixed part of my memories and feelings about that time, because of the night of her attack, because I saw her afterward. This conversation in the bar is the first time we've ever discussed her attack explicitly. But I know that, in my inner world, our friendship somehow flows from that night, from that time, because that is when she made a permanent mark on me.

In the bar in Queens, I don't know how to deal with this gap between our memories. It's *her* story, *her* attack. I feel like a thief, holding information that is not mine.

I'm torn between telling her everything and keeping it all away from her. What if she needs that fog to be her memory? What if it's a tool for self-preservation, a veil acting as a bandage? She's moved on with her life—moving to two different cities, getting a prestigious scholarship to a prestigious graduate program, expanding.

All choice is gone when she asks, "Do you know what happened to me?"

I tell her I was there afterward, that Peter and I brought her back upstairs. She doesn't react to the news of my presence, but the detail about Peter shocks her. She'd swapped him out for someone else, another tall man with longish hair, another activist but one she knew less well.

"Peter?"

Her voice is louder. The barman is looking at us with curiosity as he dries some pint glasses with a white cloth. I think he might move closer to us, but he doesn't.

"But I saw him, all these times afterward, and we were always joking, as if none of that had happened. Peter? Are you sure?"

The label on my beer is almost gone.

She wants to know more.

"Where were we?"

"You were on the corner of Tahrir Street. I saw you walking toward Talaat Harb, on that wide bit of sidewalk. We went into the building together."

"Me and you and Peter?"

"And Sherine, yes."

"Sherine," she says. Neither of us knows if Sherine is OK.

"So I was trying to help someone else?"

"Yes, you and Sherine both."

"What happened to the other woman?"

"I don't know."

I am trying to be limited in my answers, not to say anything that I haven't been asked for. I am unsure what consequences there might be for my friend, who is brave and direct, expressive and honest in almost every moment.

A few weeks later, she tells me she's been having nightmares, dreams, and hallucinations in which someone tells her that her body has tricked her, tricked her memory, made her unreliable, made her un-know the truth.

"In the dreams my limbs are taunting me," she says. "They ask me: how can we ever trust you again? You've forgotten everything, you're getting it all wrong."

But instead of saying she wished we had never had that conversation, she says it made her realize how important it was to be talking, to be writing, to be remembering.

"Even just once," she says.

Acknowledgments

Thank you, firstly, to everyone I interviewed for this book. Your experiences, memories, and words are its foundation.

Since I began interviewing and writing in 2014, the book has gone through many shapes. Thank you to Ursula Lindsey for seeing potential in a skeletal redraft, and Katie Baker for the right mix of encouragement and clear-eyed critique. Thank you for the conversations, ideas, and notes: Ifdal Elsaket, Brad Fox, Yasmine Shash, Sarah McNally, Jacques Testard, Aalam Wassef, and Sharif Abdel Kouddous. Thank you to Sarah Leonard, for her close-reading and her support. To Lila Abu-Lughod, Rema Hamami, and Nadera Shalhoub-Kevorkian and Columbia's Religion and the Framing of Gender Violence program.

Jessie Kindig is this book's dream editor, and I am forever thankful to her and to everyone at Verso. Thank you to Lisa Baker at Aitken Alexander, for picking up an adolescent manuscript.

Lina Attalah's ongoing conversation and warm intellect have made this book more open. Thank you to Ahdaf Soueif for setting the bar uncompromisingly high, while always lending a hand. Thank you always to my parents, and to my mother in particular,

Maha, who is the source of whatever tenacity I summoned in this project.

Omar Hamilton has been with me throughout this work, improving and saving it many times with his talented edits and with a generosity of spirit that I am lucky to share a life with.

Thank you to Rafiq and to Layla, for the joy.

Thank you to Salma Shamel, whose questions make me a better writer and, I hope, a better friend. What the hell are you doing, object?